THE PATH OF PURITY

PALI TEXT SOCIETY

Translation Series

(Extra Subscription : this is now fixed at 10s. per annum.)

VOLUMES ALREADY PUBLISHED:

1. **Psalms of the Early Buddhists,** Part I., PSALMS OF THE SISTERS, translated from the *Therī-gāthā.* By Mrs. Rhys Davids, D.Litt., M.A., Fellow of University College, London. 1909. Price 10s. net.

2. **Compendium of Philosophy,** being a translation of the *Abhidhammattha-saṅgaha.* By Shwe Zan Aung, B.A. Revised and edited by Mrs. Rhys Davids. 1910. Price 10s. net.

3. **The Mahāvaṃsa ;** or, The Great Chronicle of Ceylon. Translated into English by Wilhelm Geiger, Ph.D., Professor of Indogermanic Philology at Munich University ; assisted by Mabel Haynes Bode, Ph.D. 1912. Price 10s. net.

4. **Psalms of the Early Buddhists,** Part II., PSALMS OF THE BRETHREN, translated from the *Theragāthā,* with excerpts from the unpublished Commentary by Dhammapāla. By Mrs. Rhys Davids. 1913. Price 10s. net.

5. **Points of Controversy,** or Subjects of Discourse, translated from the *Kathā-Vatthu,* with notes from the Commentary. By Shwe Zan Aung and Mrs. Rhys Davids. 1915. Price 10s. net.

6. **Manual of a Mystic,** translated from the anonymous Pali-Singhalese MS., published (PTS, 1896) as *A Yogāvachara's Manual,* by F. L. Woodward, M.A., Principal of Mahinda College, Galle. 1916. Price 10s. net.

7. **The Book of the Kindred Sayings,** I., being a translation of *Saṃyutta Nikāya,* I. By Mrs. Rhys Davids. 1917. Price 10s. net.

8. **The Expositor,** Vol. I., being a translation of the *Atthasālinī* pp. 1–213 PTS ed. By Maung Tin, M.A. 1920. Price 10s. net.

9. **The Expositor,** Vol. II., being a translation of the *Atthasālinī* pp. 214 to end PTS ed. By Maung Tin, M.A. 1921. Price 10s. net.

10. **The Book of the Kindred Sayings,** II., being a translation of *Saṃyutta Nikāya,* II. By Mrs. Rhys Davids. 1922. Price 10s. net.

Pali Text Society
TRANSLATION SERIES, No. 11
(EXTRA SUBSCRIPTION)

THE
PATH OF PURITY

BEING

A TRANSLATION OF

BUDDHAGHOSA'S VISUDDHIMAGGA

BY

PE MAUNG TIN

TRANSLATOR OF THE "ATTHASĀLINĪ"

PART I.
OF VIRTUE (OR MORALS)

London
PUBLISHED FOR THE PALI TEXT SOCIETY
BY
THE OXFORD UNIVERSITY PRESS, AMEN CORNER, E.C.
AND AT
NEW YORK, TORONTO, MELBOURNE, AND BOMBAY

PRINTED IN GREAT BRITAIN.

PREFACE

THE present volume is a translation of the first part of Buddhaghosa's *Visuddhimagga*, the famous treatise which was, as is believed, written in Ceylon in the beginning of the fifth century A.D. Professor Lanman of Harvard University published an admirable analysis of this first part in the *American Academy of Arts and Sciences*, vol. xlix, No. 3, August, 1913. Since then ten years have passed by without our seeing the long-hoped-for American edition of the text or its translation. The Pali Text Society, which all along felt the need of a European edition of this work, could wait no longer, and recently brought out their own edition of the text. So, on the assurance of the editor, Mrs. Rhys Davids, that she saw no prospect of an American translation, I submitted my translation to the Pali Text Society. As has been explained in the Editorial Note to my translation of the *Atthasālinī*, if I had not entertained from year to year good hopes of seeing Professor Lanman's edition and translation, I would have taken up, six years ago, the translation of the *Visuddhimagga* instead of the *Atthasālinī*.

In the Afterword to her scholarly edition of the *Visuddhimagga*, Mrs. Rhys Davids has said what she had to say about the book and its author. I especially appreciate her useful list of quotations in the book from canonical and other works. I will here touch upon just one point. The *Visuddhimagga* makes reference (see Index) to the Commentaries on the Anguttara, Majjhima, and Saṃyutta. To those unacquainted with the history of the Commentaries it would thus seem that the *Visuddhimagga* was written later than these Commentaries. But, on the other hand, it is quoted by just these Commentaries on the Nikāyas as well as by the Sāmantapāsādikā and Atthasālinī, and is therefore earlier than these works. For instance, the Majjhima Commentary, which is being edited for the Pali Text Society by Professor James H. Woods, refers to it by name. When, therefore, the *Visuddhimagga* in its turn refers to the Majjhima

Commentary by name, the explanation may well be that the reference is not to the Majjhima Commentary as it has been written by Buddhaghosa, but to the original Ceylonese Commentary from which he later made his redaction. In the *Sumangalavilāsinī* also (i, 87), which is Buddhaghosa's Commentary on the Dīgha Nikāya, he refers to the Dīgha Commentary—that is, to the original Ceylonese Commentary he was recasting, or at least consulting. The same may be said of the other references in the *Visuddhimagga* to the Commentaries on the Anguttara and Samyutta. And we know that there were these original Ceylonese Commentaries and also the 'Porānas' on which Buddhaghosa based his writings. This explanation may account for the close similarity, which, as M. Nagai has pointed out in the *Journal of the Pali Text Society*, 1917-19, exists between the *Visuddhimagga* and the *Vimuttimagga*, a work by another writer. I would not, however, go to the extent of saying, as does M. Nagai, that these two works 'are one and the same work appearing in different attire.' Considering that the doctrines, called the Buddha's Word, have been preserved through the centuries by a line of teachers, whose aim is consistency in doctrinal interpretation rather than originality in striking out new paths, we may regard the *Visuddhimagga* and the *Vimuttimagga* as more or less independent works, written by men who belonged to the same school of thought—namely, the orthodox school at Anurādhapura. Final decision, however, should be postponed until we know more of Buddhaghosa's writings and the works to which he refers.

I have consulted with benefit the Burmese translation (Rangoon, 1914) by Pyī Sayadaw. And in the footnotes I have made occasional quotations from such works on the *Visuddhimagga* as the *Mahātīkā* by Dhammapāla of Ceylon and the *Ganthi* by Saddhammajotipāla of Burma. My thanks are due to Bhikkhu Sīlācāra, who was kind enough to go over my first draft translation of Chapter I; and to Mrs. Rhys Davids for her kind help in reading the proofs and for the keen interest she has taken in the translation.

PE MAUNG TIN.

EXETER COLLEGE, OXFORD,
December 10, 1922.

CONTENTS

	PAGE
PREFACE - - - - - - -	v
INTRODUCTORY DISCOURSE - - - - -	vi

CHAPTER

I. EXPOSITION OF VIRTUE - - - - 8–65
1. WHAT IS VIRTUE ? - - . - - 8
2. IN WHAT SENSE IS IT VIRTUE ? - - 9
3. WHAT ARE ITS CHARACTERISTICS, ITS ESSENCE, ITS MANIFESTATION, ITS PROXIMATE CAUSE ? - - - 10
4. WHAT ARE ITS ADVANTAGES ? - - 11
5. HOW MANY KINDS OF IT ARE THERE ? - 12
6. WHAT IS ITS CORRUPTION ? - - - 57
7. WHAT ITS PURIFICATION ? - - - 57

II. EXPOSITION OF THE ASCETIC PRACTICES - 66–95
GENERAL DISCOURSE - - - - 66
1. THE REFUSE-RAGMAN'S PRACTICE - - 70
2. THE THREE-ROBER'S PRACTICE - - 73
3. THE ALMSMAN'S PRACTICE - - - 74
4. THE HOUSE-TO-HOUSE-GOER'S PRACTICE - 76
5. THE ONE-SESSIONER'S PRACTICE - - 78
6. THE BOWL-FOODER'S PRACTICE - - 79
7. THE AFTERFOOD-REFUSER'S PRACTICE - 81
8. THE FORESTER'S PRACTICE - - - 81
9. THE TREE-ROOTMAN'S PRACTICE - - 84
10. THE OPEN-SPACER'S PRACTICE - - 86
11. THE BURNING-GROUNDER'S PRACTICE - 87
12. THE ANY-BEDDER'S PRACTICE - - 89
13. THE SITTING-MAN'S PRACTICE - - 90

OF ASCETIC AND OTHER TERMS AS MORAL TRIAD - 91
OF ASCETIC AND OTHER TERMS AS DIFFERENTIATED 92
IN GROUPS AND IN DETAIL - - - 93

THE PATH OF PURITY

Honour be to Him, the Blessed, the Saint, the Buddha Supreme

INTRODUCTORY DISCOURSE

> *" The man discreet, on virtue planted firm,*
> *In intellect and intuition trained ;*
> *The brother ardent and discriminant :*
> *'Tis he may from this tangle disembroil."*[1]

Thus it was spoken. And why was it thus spoken?
It is said that to the Blessed One then staying at Sāvatthi
there came one night a certain deva who, in order to have his
doubt removed, asked this question.—

> *" Tangle within, without, lo! in the toils*
> *Entangled is the race of sentient things.*
> *Hence would I ask thee, Gotama, of this :*
> *Who is't can from this tangle disembroil ?"*[1]

And this briefly is the meaning. By " tangle " is meant
the net of craving. For craving is like the tangle of the
network of branches of bamboo-bushes and the like, in the
sense of an intertwisting, because it arises below and above
repeatedly in connection with such objects as visible things.
And it is said to be " Tangle within, without," from the fact
of its arising within one's own and others' individualities
and what thereto appertains, in the organs subjective and
objective. Mankind is entangled in such a tangle. Just as
bamboos and the like are entangled by such tangles as bamboo-
bushes,[2] so all mankind, known as the various classes of

---

[1] *Kindred Sayings* I, 20   [2] *Read* veḷugumbajaṭādīhi

sentient beings, are entangled, enmeshed, embroiled, in that
tangle of craving—this is the meaning. [2] And because of
such entanglement, the meaning of, " Hence would I ask thee,
Gotama, of this," is to be understood thus:—Therefore I ask
thee, addressing the Blessed One by his family name, Gotama.
" Who is't can from this tangle disembroil?" means: Who is
able to disentangle this tangle which has thus entangled the
Three Elements ?[1]

Thus questioned, the Blessed One, walking in unobstructed
knowledge of all things, the Deva of devas, the Sakka of
Sakkas, the Brahmā of Brahmās, confident with the Four
Confidences, bearer of the Tenfold Strength, endowed with
unimpeded knowledge and the all-seeing eye, spake this
stanza in answer :—

> " *The man discreet, on virtue planted firm,*
> *In intellect and intuition trained ;*
> *The brother ardent and discriminant :*
> *'Tis he may from this tangle disembroil.*"

> In setting forth, according to the truth,
> The meaning of the stanza of the Sage,
> Which treats of virtue and such other things,
> I will expound the Path of Purity,
> Which rests on the strict rules of the devout
> Dwellers at the Great Minster, and contains
> Purest decisions, gladdening even those
> Who never may attain to purity
> For all their striving, though they seek it here,
> Not knowing aright the Path of Purity,
> Which holds all virtue, and is straight and safe,
> Though they to ordination have attained,
> Hard to attain in the Great Conqueror's realm.
> Devout men, whose desire is purity,
> Attend ye to the things that I relate.

Here, by " Purity " is meant Nibbāna, which is free from
all taints and exceedingly pure. The way to this purity is

---

[1] Or threefold conditions, *viz.* the world of sense, the world of form,
and the world of the formless.

the "Path of Purity." The means of its acquisition is called
the "Path." I am going to speak of that Path of Purity,
is the meaning. This Path of Purity has been set forth in
terms of simple insight in some places thus:—

> " *All things conditioned are impermanent;*
> *The which who understandeth, holdeth Ill*
> *In scorn.   This is the path of purity;* "[1]

[3] in terms of Jhāna-insight in other places thus.—

> " *He from Nibbāna is not far in whom*
> *Appear Jhāna and insight;* "[2]

in terms of kamma and so forth in some places thus.—

> " *Good will, and wisdom, mind by method trained,*
> *The highest conduct on good morals based:—*
> *This maketh mortals pure, not rank nor wealth,* "[3]

in terms of virtue and the like in other places thus:—

> " *He that in virtuous habit never fails,*
> *Hath insight, can to mystic rapture win,*
> *Who stirs up effort, puts forth all his strength,*
> *'Tis he can cross the flood so hard to pass;* "[4]

in terms of the application of mindfulness and so forth in
some places thus:—" This single way, this path, brethren,
is for the purification of beings . .   for the realization of
Nibbāna, to wit: the Four Applications of Mindfulness "[5]

And the same with the Supreme Efforts and so forth.
But here in the Blessed One's reply it has been set forth in
terms of virtue and so forth.

Thereon (*i e*, on the Blessed One's stanza) this is the
brief comment:—

" On virtue planted firm," means, being established in
virtue.   And here in this phrase one who is even now engaged
in fulfilling virtue is said to be established in virtue.   Hence
the meaning here is, being established in virtue by fulfilling

---

[1] *Dhammapada* 277.   [2] *Ib.* 372.
[3] *Kindred Sayings* I, 46.   [4] *Ib.* 76.
[5] *Dīgha Nikāya* ii, 290; *Dialogues of the Buddha* ii. 327.

it. " The man " means, the sentient being. " Discreet "
means, wise by means of wisdom born of kamma associated
with conception (in the womb) attended by the Three
Root-conditions.[1] " In intellect and intuition trained," means
cultivating concentration and insight; for here concentration
is set forth under the head of intellect (or mind), and insight
under the name of intuition (or wisdom). " Ardent " means
energetic; for energy is called ardour in the sense of causing
the corruptions to be completely burnt up. He who possesses
it is ardent. In " discriminant," wisdom is called discrimina-
tion. Endowed therewith, is the meaning. By this word
" discriminant " is indicated preserving wisdom.

In this answer wisdom comes three times. First there is
mother-wit, second there is insight-wisdom, and third there
is preserving wisdom, maintaining all functions.[2] He sees
danger in the stream of existence—this is " the brother "
(bhikkhu). " 'Tis he may from this tangle disembroil "
means: [4] Just as a man standing on the ground may lift
up a well-sharpened sword and clear away (disentangle) a
big bamboo-bush, so may the brother endowed with the six
states, to wit: this virtue and this concentration set forth
under the heading of mind, and this threefold wisdom, and
this ardour, and standing on the ground of virtue, lift up, by
means of the hand of preserving wisdom supported by the
strength of energy, the sword of insight-wisdom well sharpened
on the stone of concentration, and clear away, cleave that
entire tangle of craving which keeps falling into the continuity
of his own aggregates. And indeed he clears that tangle
at the moment of his attainment of the Path. At the moment
of Fruition he, having cleared the tangle, is worthy of the best
gifts in heaven and earth. Hence has the Blessed One said:—

> " *The man discreet, on virtue planted firm,*
> *In intellect and intuition trained;*
> *The brother ardent and discriminant:*
> *'Tis he may from this tangle disembroil.*"

---

[1] *Viz.* The absence of greed, of hate, of delusion.
[2] Such as acquiring the subjects of meditation, making frequent
questionings and being strenuous in culture.

What is meant therein is, that there remains nothing for
" the man " to do in regard to that wisdom by means of
which he is said to be " discreet," for his wisdom has been
made perfect in virtue of kamma done in a previous existence.
And in " ardent and discriminant " it is meant that he is to
be persevering by means of the said energy, and compre-
hending by means of wisdom; and establishing himself in
virtue, cultivate calm and insight indicated by way of
intellect (or mind) and intuition (or wisdom). Here, thus,
the Blessed One has set forth this Path of Purity under the
heads of virtue, concentration, and wisdom.

Indeed, thus far have been set forth the threefold training,
the religion happy in its three stages,[1] the sufficing condition
of the threefold knowledge[2] and so forth, the avoidance of the
two extremes and the practice of the middle course, the means
of escaping states of woe and so forth, the rejection of the
corruptions in three ways, the opposition to transgression and
so forth, the cleansing from the three corruptions, and the
instrumentality necessary to Stream-winning and so forth.

How so ? Here by virtue is indicated the training in the
higher virtue; by concentration, the training in the higher
thought; and by wisdom, the training in the higher wisdom.

And by virtue is indicated the happiness of the religion in
its beginning. For, from such expressions as: " *What is the
beginning of moral states ? The virtue of great purity,*"[3] and
" *the refraining from all evil,*"[4] it is evident that virtue is the
beginning of the religion. And since it bears such merit as
absence of remorse, it is happy.

By concentration is indicated the happiness of the religion
in its progress. [5] For, from such expressions as: " *the
fulfilment of morality,*"[4] and so on, it is evident that concentration is in the middle of the religion. And since it bears such
merit as the various kinds of supra-normal power, it is happy.

By wisdom is indicated the happiness of the religion in its

---

[1] Its beginning, progress, and end.
[2] Knowledge of former existences, the passing away and reappearing
of beings, and the destruction of the intoxicants.
[3] *Saṃyutta* v, 143.   [4] *Dhammapada* 183.

consummation. For, from the expression, "*the cleansing of one's mind, . . . this is the religion of the Buddhas,*"[1] we see the superiority of wisdom, and that it is the consummation of the religion. And since it maintains its natural state unaffected amid desirable and undesirable things, it is happy.

As it has been said:—

> "*As wind a massy rock doth never move,
> So neither praise nor dispraise moves the wise.*"[2]

Similarly, in virtue is set forth the sufficing condition of endowment with the Threefold Knowledge. For, depending on the attainment of virtue one attains to the Threefold Knowledge, and not to anything higher. In concentration is set forth the sufficing condition of endowment with the Sixfold Superknowledge.[3] For, depending on the fulfilment of concentration one attains to the Sixfold Superknowledge, and not to anything higher. And in wisdom is set forth the sufficing condition of the various kinds of analysis. For, depending on the attainment of wisdom and on no other ground, one attains to the Four Analyses.[4]

By virtue also is indicated the avoiding of the extreme of devotion to the pleasures of sensuality; by concentration the avoiding of the extreme of self-mortification; and by wisdom the practising of the middle course.

Similarly in virtue is set forth the means of transcending the states of woe; in concentration the means of transcending the elements of sensuality; and in wisdom the means of transcending all existences.

Again, by virtue is set forth the rejection of the corruptions by way of partial rejection;[5] by concentration, that by way of

---

[1] *Dhammapada* 183.　　　　　　　　　　[2] *Ib.* 81.

[3] Super-normal power of (1) manipulating the physical form, (2) clairaudience far and near, (3) knowing others' thoughts, (4) remembering former existences, (5) clairvoyance far and near, (6) knowing how to bring the intoxicants to an end.

[4] Analysis of things, causes, terms, and the knowing process.

[5] *Tadangappahāna :* 'rejection by parts,' rejection of various parts of immorality by various parts of morality, as darkness by the light of a lamp. Translated as 'elimination of the factor in question' in *Expositor* 454.

discarding; and by wisdom, that by way of extermination.

Again, by virtue is set forth opposition to actual deeds of the corruptions; by concentration, opposition to their uprising; by wisdom, opposition to their latent tendency.

[6] Again, by virtue is set forth the cleansing of the corruption of misconduct; by concentration, cleansing of the corruption of craving; by wisdom, cleansing of the corruption of views.

Again, by virtue is set forth the instrumentality for Stream-winning and Once-returning; by concentration, that for Never-returning; and by wisdom, that for Sanctity. For the Stream-winner is said to be a fulfiller of virtue; likewise the Once-returner. But the Never-returner is said to be a fulfiller of concentration; and the Saint a fulfiller of wisdom.

Thus in so far are set forth these nine triads, to wit; the Threefold Training, the religion happy in its three stages, the sufficing condition of the Threefold Knowledge and so forth, the avoidance of the two extremes and the practice of the middle course, the means of transcending the states of woe and so forth, the rejection of the corruptions in three ways, the opposition to transgression and so forth, the cleansing of the three corruptions, the instrumentality for Stream-winning and so forth, and such other triads as those of merits.

This is the Introductory Discourse.

CHAPTER I

EXPOSITION OF VIRTUE

THUS this Path of Purity, albeit set forth under the heads of virtue, concentration, and wisdom, including various merits, has been expounded very briefly indeed. Consequently it may not be sufficiently useful to all; and so, in order to make it known in detail, the following questions are asked, beginning with the subject of virtue:—

1. What is virtue?[1] 2. In what sense is it virtue? 3. What are its characteristics, its essence, its manifestation, its proximate cause? 4. What are its advantages? 5. How many kinds of virtue are there? 6. What is its corruption? 7. And what its purification?

And these are the answers:—

1. What is virtue?

Such states as the volition of one who abstains from life-taking and so forth, or of one who fulfils his set duties. For, this has been said in the Paṭisambhidāmagga,[2] "*What is virtue? Volition is virtue; mental properties are virtue; restraint* [7] *is virtue; non-transgression is virtue;*" wherein the volition which is virtue is that of one who abstains from life-taking and so forth, or of one who fulfils his set duties; and the mental properties which are virtue are the abstinence of one who abstains from life-taking and so forth. Further, the volition which is virtue is that of the seven courses of action of one who forsakes life-taking, and so on; the mental properties which are virtue are such states as non-covetous-

---

[1] Sīla is moral habit, habitual good conduct. *Cf. Pss. of the Brethren*, p. 269, n. 2. It was the very essence of the Founder's gospel. For his Order it became the basis of doctrine, and elaborated into what we understand by virtue.

[2] i, 44.

8

ness, goodwill, right views expressed in this manner: " Putting away covetousness he lives by thought free from covetousness." In " restraint is virtue," restraint should be understood as fivefold:[1] by means of the Pātimokkha, of mindfulness, of knowledge, of patience, of energy. Of these, " *He is endowed, fulfilled with this restraint according to the Pātimokkha*"[2] —this is Pātimokkha-restraint. " *He keeps watch over the controlling faculty of sight, attains to the restraint of the controlling faculty of sight*,"[3]—this is mindfulness-restraint.

> " *The currents flowing in the world O Ajita,*
> *Said the Exalted One, these may*
> *By mindfulness be checked, this the restraint I teach,*
> *By insight they may be shut in.*"[4]

—this is knowledge-restraint in which (knowledge in) the (right) use of the (four) requisites also is included. " *One endures cold and heat* "[5]—in such expressions it is patience-restraint. " *One does not consent to the uprisen lustful thought* "[6] —in such expressions it is energy-restraint, in which purity of livelihood also is included. Thus this Fivefold Restraint as well as the restraint which noble youths dreading sin exercise in regard to anything that falls in their way should be understood as restraint-virtue. " Non-transgression is virtue," means the absence of bodily and vocal transgression in one practised in virtue. This so far is the answer to the question, " What is virtue ?"

[8] Passing to the remaining questions:

2. In what sense is it virtue ?

It is virtue in the sense of being virtuous (or moral). And what is this ? The being virtuous, is the right placing together (of bodily and vocal actions). The meaning is that because one is highly virtuous, one's bodily actions and so on are not dissipated. Or it means, supporting. The being a

---

[1] See also *Expositor* 454, where ' restraint by virtue ' is synonymous with Pātimokkha-restraint.

[2] *Vibhanga* 246. [3] *Dīgha* i, 70. [4] *Sutta Nipāta* 1035.
[5] *Majjhima* i, 10. [6] *Ib.* 11.

support of moral states by way of establishment, is the meaning. Indeed those who are skilful in the significations of words here understand this double meaning. But others set forth the meaning in such ways as: "It is virtue in the sense of being the head (*sira*), in the sense of being cool (*sīta*)."

3. Now: What are its characteristics, its essence, its manifestation, its proximate cause?

> So has it been divided, and its mark
> Is virtue, even as visibility[1]
> The mark of objects is.

For just as visibility is the characteristic mark of the different varieties of form such as indigo, yellow, and so on, because albeit of such various kinds they do not go beyond visibility, so what has been said about being virtuous by way of the right placing of bodily actions and so forth, and of the establishment of moral states, is the characteristic mark of the different varieties of virtue such as volition and so on, because, notwithstanding its various kinds, it does not go beyond right placing and establishment. And concerning virtue, as possessing such a characteristic, this has been said:—

> Her active property or essence lies
> In excellence and war against all sin.

Therefore this virtue possesses the essence, in the sense of function, of destroying wickedness; and has the essence, in the sense of property, of faultlessness. For when the characteristics and so on are mentioned, essence is said to be either function or property.

> It manifests itself as purity;
> Its proximate cause is the sense of shame
> And dread of blame (for so the wise give praise).

[9] This virtue has, as its manifestation, purity, said to be purity of body, of speech, and of mind. It is considered to

---

[1] *Read* sanidassanattaṁ—perception of form, that is, perception of objects through the visual sense, is, for all that sense *by itself* can tell us, perception of various colour-areas and nothing more.

manifest itself as purity. Sense of shame and dread of blame are extolled by the wise as its proximate cause, which means immediate reason. For in the presence of sense of shame and dread of blame, virtue arises and establishes itself: in their absence it does not arise nor establish itself. Thus are to be understood its characteristic, essence, manifestation, and proximate cause.

4. What are its advantages?

The acquirement of various qualities such as absence of remorse. For it has been said, "*Ānanda, moral virtues have absence of remorse for benefit and advantage.*"[1] Further, "*Householders, five are the advantages of the fulfilment of virtue obtained by the virtuous. What are these five advantages? In this world, householders, one virtuous, endowed with virtue, acquires much wealth chiefly owing to the effect of non-negligence. This is the first advantage of the fulfilment of virtue by the virtuous. Again, householders, of one virtuous, endowed with virtue, a good report is noised abroad. This is the second advantage of the fulfilment of virtue by the virtuous. Again, householders, to whatsoever assembly one virtuous, endowed with virtue, goes, he enters boldly and unperturbed, whether it be an assembly of princes, an assembly of brahmins, an assembly of laymen, or an assembly of monks. This is the third advantage of the fulfilment of virtue by the virtuous. Again, householders, one virtuous, endowed with virtue, dies undeluded. This is the fourth advantage of the fulfilment of virtue by the virtuous. Again, householders, one virtuous, endowed with virtue, on the dissolution of the body after death, reaches a happy destiny, a heavenly world. This is the fifth advantage of the fulfilment of virtue by the virtuous.*"[2]

Furthermore: "*Brethren, should a brother desire to be dear and precious to, respected and honoured by his fellow-monks, he should fulfil the virtues.*"[3]—In such wise have the various advantages of virtue, beginning with loveableness and preciousness and ending in the destruction of the intoxicants, been mentioned. Thus various qualities such as absence

---

[1] *Anguttara* v, 1.   [2] *Digha* ii, 86.   [3] *Majjhima* i, 33.

of remorse constitute the advantages of virtue. [10] Moreover:—

> The true religion gives to noble sons
> No other stay than virtue. Who can tell
> The limit of her power ? Not Gangā stream
> Nor Yamunā nor babbling Sarabhū,
> Nor Aciravatī nor Mahī's flood,
> Can purify on earth the taints of men.
> But virtue's water can remove the stain
> Of all things living. Necklaces or pearl,
> Rain-bearing breezes, yellow sandalwood,
> Gems, nor soft rays of moonlight can destroy
> Heart-burnings of a creature. She alone—
> Virtue—well-guarded, noble, cool, avails.
> What scent else blows with and against the wind ?
> What stairway leads like her to heaven's gate ?
> What door into Nibbāna's city opes ?
> The Sage whose virtue is his ornament
> Outshines the pomp and pearls of jewelled kings.
> In virtuous men[1] virtue destroys self-blame,
> Begetting joy and praise. Thus should be known
> The sum of all the discourse on the power
> Of virtue, root of merits, slayer of faults.

Now this is the answer to—

5. How many kinds of it are there ?

(i) All this virtue is of one kind through its characteristic
of being virtuous (monad i.).

(ii) It is of two kinds as positive or negative rules of
conduct (dyad 1); likewise as the minor or the major precepts[2]
(dyad 2); as abstinence or non-abstinence (dyad 3); as interested or disinterested (dyad 4); as practised for a limited
period of life or until the end of life (dyad 5); as violable or
inviolable (dyad 6); as worldly or transcendental (dyad 7).

[11] (iii) It is of three kinds as inferior, middling or
superior (triad 1); likewise as dominantly influenced by self,

---

[1] *Note the plural form* yatino *instead of* yatayo.
[2] *Or,* the specialized or fundamental precepts.

by the world, or by the Law[1] (triad 2); as misconstrued, not misconstrued, or tranquillized (triad 3); as pure, impure, or doubtful (triad 4); as probationary, adept, or neither probationary nor adept (triad 5).

(iv) It is of four kinds as partaking of deterioration, of stability, of speciality, or of penetration (tetrad 1); likewise as concerning the brethren, concerning the sisters, concerning novices, or concerning laymen (tetrad 2); as natural, customary practice, fixed law, or the fruit of former conditions (tetrad 3); and as restraint according to the Pâtimokkha, restraint of the controlling faculties, purity of livelihood, or connected with the requisites (tetrad 4).

(v) It is of five kinds as limited precepts of purity, unlimited precepts of purity, completed precepts of purity, precepts of purity not misconstrued, or tranquillized precepts of purity, according to what has been said in the Paṭisambhidā (pentad 1); likewise as rejection, abstention, volition, restraint, or non-transgression (pentad 2).

Of these,

(i) In the onefold portion (monad 1) the meaning is to be understood as has been said above.[2]

(ii) In the twofold portion (dyad 1) the fulfilling of the precepts enacted by the Blessed One thus: "This ought to be practised," is a positive rule of conduct; the non-doing of what has been prohibited as, "This ought not to be practised," is a negative rule of conduct. Here is the word-definition: by having fulfilled the precepts those who are endowed with a precept *are practised* in it—'positive rule of conduct.' By means of it they avoid, guard against a *prohibition*—'negative rule of conduct.' Of these two, the former is accomplished by the effort of faith, the latter by faith. Thus it is twofold as positive and negative rules of conduct.

In the second dyad special precept means the highest precept. 'Specialized' is just special. Or, what is enacted with reference to a special precept is the 'specialized precept,' a synonym for the precept which remains over from the set

---

[1] Dhamma   [2] P. 9

of eight precepts of which pure livelihood is the eighth.[1]
' The fundamental precept ' is the foundation of the exalted
practice of the Path; and is a synonym for the set of eight
precepts of which pure livelihood is the eighth. This set of
eight is the foundation of the Path, because it ought to be in
purified practice previous to the Path. Hence (the Buddha)
has said: " *Previously his bodily action, his vocal action, his
livelihood have been well purified.*"[2] Or, what has been declared
to be the minor and lesser precepts, [12] is the " minor precept." The remainder is the " major precept." Or, that
which is included in both the Vibhanga's,[3] is the " major
precept "; that which is included in the Khandhaka[4] duties
is the " minor precept." The former is perfected by perfec-
tion in the latter. Hence (the Buddha) has said: " *Brethren,
it is impossible that a brother without fulfilling the law of the
minor precept, should fulfil the law of the major precept.*"[5]
Thus it is twofold, as minor and major precepts (or specialized
and fundamental).

In the third dyad, the mere abstention from life-taking
and so on, is the virtue of abstinence. The remaining volition
and so on, is the virtue of non-abstinence. Thus it is twofold
as abstinence and non-abstinence.

In the fourth dyad ' interested ' means that there are two
inducements: the inducement of craving and the inducement of
views. Of these two that which arises from a desire to attain
(a blissful) existence thus: " *By means of this virtue I shall
become a deva or a certain deva,*"[6] is the inducement of craving.
That which arises from pure views thus: " *By means of this
virtue there will be purity,*"[7] is the inducement of views. And
there is the transcendental virtue, and there is the worldly
virtue which is a constituent of this—these constitute the

---

[1] *Viz.* the purified actions, three of deed and four of speech, and pure
livelihood. *Cf. Expositor* 505.

[2] *Cf. Anguttara* iii, 124 *f.*

[3] *I.e.* precepts for the brethren and the sisters as laid down in the
Pātimokkha, *Vinaya Texts* i (Sacred Books of the East).

[4] *I.e.* in the Mahāvagga and Cullavagga, *Ib.* i, ii, iii.

[5] *Anguttara* iii, 14.   [6] *Ib.* iv, 461.   [7] *Dhammasangani* 1005

" disinterested virtue." Thus it is twofold, as interested and disinterested.

In the fifth dyad the virtue which is practised within a time-limit is " for a limited period of life." That which arises so long as it is practised during a life-time is ' until the end of life.' Thus it is twofold, as practised for a limited period of life, and until the end of life.

In the sixth dyad that which is limited by present gain, pomp, relatives, limbs and life, is known as " violable." What is contrary to that is " inviolable." And this has been said in the Paṭisambhidā:[1] ' *What is that virtue which is violable? There is virtue violable by gain, there is virtue violable by pomp, there is virtue violable by relatives, there is virtue violable by limbs, there is virtue violable by life. What is that virtue which is violable by gain? Some one in the world on account of, by reason of, for the sake of gain transgresses any precept that may have been observed. Such* [13] *is the virtue that is violable by gain.*' In this way the others also should be expanded. In the answers concerning the inviolable, also, it has been said:[2] " *What is that virtue which is not violable by gain? In this world, on account of, by reason of, for the sake of gain, a certain person does not give rise even to a thought of transgressing any precept that may have been observed. How, then, will he transgress it? Such virtue is not violable by gain.*" In this way also the others should be expanded. Thus it is twofold, as violable and as inviolable.

In the seventh dyad all virtue which is accompanied by (or the object of) the intoxicants is " worldly "; that which is not accompanied by the intoxicants is " transcendental." Of these two worldly virtue brings about distinction in present life, and is a constituent part of the escape from existence. As has been said:[3] " *Discipline is for the purpose of restraint, which is for the purpose of absence of remorse, which is for the purpose of gladness, which is for the purpose of rapture, which is for the purpose of repose, which is for the purpose of bliss, which is for the purpose of concentration, which is for the purpose*

---

[1] i, 43.   [2] *Ib.* i, 44.   [3] *Vinaya* v, 164.

of knowing and seeing the truth, which is for the purpose of disgust, which is for the purpose of dispassion, which is for the purpose of emancipation, which is for the purpose of knowing and seeing emancipation, which is for the purpose of birthless Parinibbāna.[1] *For such purpose is the discourse (on the Discipline), for such purpose is the consultation, for such purpose is the groundwork, for such purpose is the attentiveness, namely, the emancipation of the mind devoid of grasping.*" Transcendental virtue brings about escape from existence, and is the ground of retrospective knowledge. Thus it is twofold, as worldly and transcendental.

(iii) Among the triads: In the first triad, that virtue which arises through inferior conation, consciousness, energy, or investigation, is " inferior "; that through middling conation and so on is "middling "; that through superior conation and so on is " superior." Or, that which is practised from a desire for pomp is " inferior "; that for a meritorious result is "middling"; that which is practised in connection with Ariyanship,[2] thus: " This is what ought to be done,"[3] is " superior." Or, virtue corrupted by exalting self and disparaging others, thus: " I am possessed of virtue; but these other brethren are wicked and evil in nature," is " inferior "; worldly virtue uncorrupted is " middling "; transcendental virtue is " superior." Or, that virtue which arises for the sake of wealth and property by way of craving is " inferior "; that for the sake of self-emancipation is " middling "; while that virtue of the perfections which arises for the sake of the emancipation of all beings, is " superior." Thus, it is threefold as inferior, middling, and superior.

In the second triad that virtue which arises out of self-respect, having regard for self, and from a desire to put away what is improper for self, [14] is " dominantly influenced

---

[1] Anupādāparinibbāna, *i.e.* entrance into Nibbāna which, not grasping after anything, leaves no material form behind and does not give rise to rebirth.

[2] On the definition of *Ariyan* see *Expositor* 452.

[3] *The Ṭīkā reads:* in connection with Ariyanship out of a loathing for evil: ' How shall one like me do such evil ?'

by self." That which arises out of respect for the world, having regard for the world, and from a desire to avoid accusation by the world, is " dominantly influenced by the world." That which arises out of respect for the Law, having regard for the Law, and from a desire to honour the greatness of the Law, is " dominantly influenced by the Law." Thus it is threefold as dominantly influenced by self, and so on.

In the third triad that virtue which in the dyads (dyad 4) was said to be ' interested,' is ' misconstrued ' through the misconstruction of craving and views. That virtue which is a constituent part of the path of a good average person and which is associated with the path of the probationers, is ' not misconstrued.' That which is associated with the fruition of probation and adeptship is " tranquillized." Thus it is threefold as misconstrued and so on.

In the fourth triad that virtue which is fulfilled without committing an offence or by atoning for an offence committed, is " pure "; the virtue of one who has not atoned for an offence committed is " impure "; the virtue of one who has doubts regarding the object, the offence, or the transgression, is known as " doubtful." Of these, the religious meditator should purify the impure virtue; and when there is doubt, it should be dispelled by not transgressing against the object. So will it be pleasant for him. Thus it is threefold as pure, and so on.

In the fifth triad virtue associated with the four Ariyan Paths and the three fruitions of monkhood is " probationary "; that which is associated with the fruition of sanctity is " adept "; the rest is " neither probationary nor adept." Thus it is threefold as probationary, and so on. But virtue is spoken of as simply the natural dispositions of the various beings in the world, so that, as referring to their virtue, one speaks of a man who has a disposition for ease, of one who has a disposition for ill, of one who has a disposition for quarrels, of one who has a disposition for beautification; thus, therefore, in the Paṭisambhidā[1] there are three kinds of virtue: moral, immoral, and unmoral. Hence it is said to be threefold, as moral,

---

[1] i, 44.

and so on. Of these three, immoral virtue does not correspond
to any of the characteristics of the virtue which is meant here,
therefore this triad has not been brought in here. Hence the
division of the triads is to be understood in accordance with
the method here given.

(iv) In the first of the tetrads:—

> Who serveth here the wicked, not the good,
> Seeth no injury to anything,
> Because he is unwise. [15] Full of wrong thoughts,
> He heeds not the controlling faculties,
> And all his virtue to corruption turns.
> Who is content with his own virtue won,
> Nor will bestir him to apply his mind
> In stations of religious exercise,
> Pleased with his virtue, seeking nothing higher,—
> This brother's virtue turns to stagnancy.
> The virtuous, seeking fixity of thought,—
> His virtue to pre-eminence is turned.
> Dissatisfied, wrapped in world-weariness,—
> This brother's virtue is to insight turned.

Thus it is fourfold as partaking of deterioration, and so on.

In the second tetrad there are precepts enacted for the
brethren, who should keep them separate from those enacted
for the sisters. This is virtue " concerning the brethren."
There are precepts enacted for the sisters, who should keep
them separate from those enacted for the brethren. This is
virtue " concerning the sisters." The ten precepts for novices
male and female constitute virtue " concerning novices."
There are five precepts—ten if possible—for the constant
practice of lay-disciples, male and female. Eight are by way
of duties for the sacred day. These constitute virtue " concerning laymen." Thus it is fourfold as concerning the
brethren, and so on.

In the third tetrad non-transgression by men of Uttara-
kuru[1] is " natural " virtue. The regulated conduct of various
people according to family customs, localities, beliefs, is

---

[1] One of the ' four Great Islands.'

virtue "as customary practice." The virtue of the mother of the future Buddha, declared thus: "*This is a fixed law, Ānanda, that when the future Buddha descended into the mother's womb, she had no thought connected with lust for men,*"[1] is virtue "as fixed law." The virtue of such pure beings as Mahākassapa, and others, and of the future Buddha in many births, is virtue "as the fruit of former conditions." Thus it is fourfold as natural, and so on.

In the fourth tetrad, (*a*) that virtue which has been declared by the Blessed One thus: "*Here (in this religion) a brother lives, being restrained by the restraint of the Pātimokkha, is possessed of good behaviour and lawful resort, sees danger in the smallest faults, trains himself in the observance of the precepts*"[2]—this is virtue "as restraint according to the Pātimokkha." (*b*) Virtue "as restraint of the controlling faculties," is that virtue which has been declared thus: "*When he sees an object with his eye,* [16] *he is not entranced by the general appearance or the details of it. He sets himself to restrain that which might give occasion for immoral states, covetousness, and grief to flow in over him while he dwells unrestrained as to the faculty of sight. He keeps watch over his faculty of sight, and he attains to mastery over it. And so, in like manner, when he hears a sound with his ear, or smells an odour with his nose, or tastes a flavour with his tongue, or feels a touch with his body, or cognizes an idea with his mind, he is not entranced by the general appearance or the details of it. He sets himself to restrain that which might give occasion for immoral states, covetousness, and grief to flow in over him while he dwells unrestrained as to the faculty of mind. He keeps watch over his mental (representative) faculty, and he attains to mastery over it.*"[3] (*c*) The abstinence from wrong livelihood arisen by way of evil states, such as the transgression of the six precepts enacted for the sake of livelihood, and as "trickery, boastful talk (about self and donors), insinuation (in almsgiving), crushing slander, hungering to add gain to gain,"[4] is virtue "as purity of livelihood." (*d*) The use of the four requisites

---

[1] *Majjhima* iii, 121.   [2] *Vibhanga* 244.   [3] *Dīgha* i, 70.
[4] *Vibhanga* 345. *Cf. Dialogues of the Buddha* i, 15.

after pure reflection set forth after this manner: "*He accepts the robe wisely reflecting that it is only for the warding off of cold*,"[1] is known as virtue " connected with the requisites."

5 (iv, a). Virtue as restraint according to the Pātimokkha.

Herein (*i.e.* dealing with the four kinds of the fourth tetrad) this is the deciding discourse together with the word-by-word comment from the beginning: "Here" means, "in this religion." "Brother" is a son of respectable family, who from faith becomes a monk in the customary way, because of his *viewing danger* in the stream of existence, or of wearing torn shattered rags, and so forth. In " being restrained by the restraint of the Pātimokkha," "Pātimokkha" is the virtue of the precepts. It *delivers*, releases him who *guards* it, observes it, from the ills of the states of woe and so forth— hence it is called "Pātimokkha." The restraining is " restraint," a name for non-transgression, bodily and vocal. " The restraint of the Pātimokkha" means that the Pāti- mokkha itself is the restraint. "Being restrained by the restraint of the Pātimokkha" means, to be restrained by that Pātimokkha-restraint. Attained to, endowed with, is the meaning. "Lives" means comports himself.

[17] The meaning of, "is possessed of good behaviour and lawful resort," and so on, is to be understood in the way that comes in the Pali text.[2] For this has been said: '*He is possessed of good behaviour and lawful resort. There is good behaviour and there is misbehaviour. Of these what is misbe- haviour? Bodily transgression, vocal transgression, bodily- and-vocal transgression, this is called misbehaviour. All wickedness also is misbehaviour. A certain member of the Order here obtains his livelihood by a gift of bamboos, of leaves, of flowers, or fruits, or bath-powder, or tooth-sticks, by fawning, by bean-curry talk, by nurture (of supporters' chil- dren), by carrying messages on foot, or by any other means of wrong livelihood loathed by the Buddhas. This is called misbehaviour.*

---

[1] *Majjhima* i, 10. The remaining portion of this quotation is brought out and commented on in p. 36 *f.*

[2] *Vibhanga* 246.

And what is good behaviour? Bodily non-transgression, vocal non-transgression, bodily-and-vocal non-transgression— this is called good behaviour. All virtue-restraint also is good behaviour. A certain member of the Order here does not obtain his livelihood by a gift of bamboos . . . loathed by the Buddhas. This is called good behaviour. As regards lawful resort—there is lawful resort, and there is unlawful resort. Of these, what is unlawful resort? A certain member of the Order here resorts (for alms) to a harlot, a widow, an old maid, a eunuch, a nun, or a liquor shop; against the precepts, he associates after the manner of laymen, with kings, ministers, heretical teachers, and their disciples; serves, follows, attends on families of faithless unbelievers, who abuse and censure the brethren and sisters, the lay-disciples male and female, not wishing their good, benefit, comfort or security (from the burden of ill). [18] This is called unlawful resort. And what is lawful resort? A certain member of the Order here does not resort to a harlot . . . does not associate after the manner of laymen, against the precepts, with kings . . . serves, follows, attends on faithful families of believers who are welling springs (for the benefit of monks), who love the shining of yellow robes and the odour of sanctity, and who desire the good, benefit, comfort, and security of the brethren and sisters, of the lay-disciples male and female. This is called lawful resort. Thus being full of, fulfilled with, arrived at, attained to, possessed of, fully possessed of, endowed with such good behaviour and such lawful resort, one is said to be " possessed of good behaviour and lawful resort." '

Further, " good behaviour and lawful resort " here should be understood also in this way: For misbehaviour is twofold, bodily and vocal. Of these what is bodily misbehaviour? A certain member of the Order here, having gone to an assembly of the Order, stands and sits rudely brushing against the senior brethren; stands and sits in front; sits on a high seat; sits with his head covered; speaks while standing and while stretching out his arm; walks up and down with sandals on while the senior brethren walk without sandals; walks above while they walk below; walks on the promenade while they walk on the ground; stands and sits pushing himself close to the senior brethren; withholds seats from the new brethren; without the permission of the senior brethren throws down fire-wood in the fire-shed and shuts its door; goes down to the bathing-place brushing against the senior brethren and before them; takes a bath brushing against them and before them; comes up brushing against them and before them; enters among houses brushing against them and before them; departing from their side goes in front of them; enters abruptly into the secret and private rooms of respectable people, where their women and daughters are sitting down, and strokes the head of a child. This is called bodily misbehaviour.

And what is vocal misbehaviour ? A certain member of the Order here goes to an assembly of the Order, and without asking leave of the senior brethren rudely speaks on the Law, answers a question and expounds the Pātimokkha; speaks while standing, [19] and while stretching out his arm; goes among houses, and says to a woman or a girl: "Madam so-and-so, of such and such a family, what is there to eat and drink ? Is there rice-gruel ? Is there food ? Is there something to eat ? What shall we drink ? What shall we eat ? Of what shall we partake ? What will you give me ?" Thus he chatters. This is called vocal misbehaviour. Good behaviour should be understood as its opposite. Furthermore, a brother is respectful, obedient, possessed of a sense of shame and dread of blame, wears his inner and outer robes properly, is distinguished by his gracious manner of advancing, of retreating, of looking ahead, of looking sideways, of bending and stretching his limbs, keeps his eyes lowered, is possessed of good deportment, keeps a guarded door as respects his controlling faculties, is moderate in food, devoted to keeping awake, endowed with mindfulness and comprehension, free from desires, contented, strenuously energetic, a respectful observer of the minor precepts, and full of regard for worthy things. This is called good behaviour. So far it should be understood.

Lawful resort is of three kinds: as a sufficing condition, as a guardian, and as a bond. Of these what is lawful resort as a sufficing condition ? A good friend endowed with the qualities of the ten subjects of discourse, owing to whom one hears what has not hitherto been heard, purifies what has been heard, gets beyond one's doubts, rectifies one's views and composes one's mind; or under whose training one increases in faith, virtue, learning, self-sacrifice, wisdom, is called lawful resort as a sufficing condition.

What is lawful resort as a guardian ? A brother here, on entering among the houses of a village and walking along the streets, goes lowering his eyes, looking before him not further than the distance of a plough, and is well-restrained. He does not go looking at an elephant, a horse, a chariot, a pedestrian, a woman, or a man. He does not go looking above, down, or in different directions. This is called lawful resort as a guardian.

What is lawful resort as a bond ? The four applications of mindfulness[1] wherein the mind is bound. For this has been said by the Blessed One: " *Brethren, what is the lawful resort of a brother, his paternal province ? It is the four applications of mindfulness.*"[2] This is called lawful resort as a bond. Thus being full of . . . endowed with such good behaviour and lawful resort, one is said to be " possessed of good behaviour and lawful resort."

[20] " Sees danger in the smallest faults "—is in the habit of seeing danger in the various kinds of the smallest faults, such as are unintentional, committed in the course of his training, produced by immoral states of consciousness.

" Trains himself in the observance of the precepts "— trains himself by observing all that ought to be observed in the precepts. And here by so much of the text " being restrained by the restraint of the Pātimokkha," the virtue of the Pātimokkha-restraint is indicated by the exposition, determined by the person. But all beginning with " is possessed of good behaviour and lawful resort " should be understood to have been said to indicate that practice which arises for any one who practises it.

---

[1] *I.e.* as regards the body, feelings, thought, and states.

[2] *Saŋyutta* v, 148.

5 (iv, *b*). Virtue as restraint of the Controlling Faculties.

In virtue as restraint of the Controlling Faculties which has been shown in this way, " when he sees an object with his eye," and so on (p. 19), " He " is a brother established in virtue which is of the-Pātimokkha-restraint.

" When (he) sees an object with his eye,"—when he sees an object by means of visual cognition commonly called the eye as instrument, and capable of seeing an object. But the Ancients have said: " The eye does not see the object in the absence of the mind. The mind does not see the object in the absence of the eye. But one sees by the mind with the sentient eye as basis, when an impact takes place between the door (of the eye) and the object." Nevertheless, such a discourse as the present one really refers to the constituent parts of sight in the same sense as when one says, " He pierces with a bow," and so forth. Therefore the meaning here is, " when he sees an object by visual cognition."

" Is not entranced by the general appearance,"—does not seize the general appearance as furnishing a basis for corruption, such as the general appearance of a woman, a man, or of any desirable form, and so on. He stops at what is actually seen. " Is not entranced by the details of it,"—does not seize the different modes of hand, foot, smiling, laughing, speaking, looking ahead, looking sideways, and so forth, which have obtained the common name of " details " by reason of repeated expression as a manifestation of the corruptions. He seizes only what appears (as the abominable thirty-two parts) in the body, like Mahātissa the Elder who lived at Mount Cetiya. It is said that a certain daughter-in-law, having broken with her husband and having well beautified and dressed herself like a celestial nymph, left Anurādhapura betimes, and, while going to the home of her relatives, saw on the way the Elder, who was coming to Anurādhapura from Mount Cetiya for the sake of alms, and with corrupt thoughts [21] laughed aloud. The Elder, wondering what it was, looked up, and acquiring the perception of the foul in her teeth (-bones), attained Sanctity. Hence it has been said:—

"Those bones, her teeth, he saw, and called to mind
His first perception. Even where he stood
The Elder thus attained to Sanctity."

And the husband, following the same road, saw the Elder
and enquired: "Perhaps Your Reverence has met a certain
lady?" The Elder replied:—

"I know not whether man or woman passed.
A certain lump of bones went by this way."

In "which might give occasion," and so on, these states
such as covetousness and so forth might flow in over, might
pursue this person who dwells with the door of his sight open
without shutting the faculty of sight by the door-leaf of mindfulness on account of, by reason of, whatsoever non-restraint
of the faculty of sight. "He sets himself to restrain that,"—
sets himself to shut his faculty of sight by the door-leaf of
mindfulness. Only he who is practising thus is said "to keep
watch over his faculty of sight and to attain to mastery over
it," whereby, if there is neither restraint nor non-restraint in
the faculty of sight, it is because there arises neither mindfulness nor forgetfulness with reference to the sentient eye.
But indeed, when a visible object enters the avenue of sight,
then, on the cessation of the subconsciousness after arising
two or three times, the inoperative mind-element (or, the
five-door-adverting) arises, accomplishing the function of
adverting, and then ceases. Then arise and cease in order,
the visual cognition accomplishing the function of seeing,
the resultant mind-element accomplishing the function of
receiving, the resultant element of mind-cognition without
root-conditions accomplishing the function of scrutinizing,
and the inoperative element of mind-cognition without root-
conditions accomplishing the function of determining.
Immediately afterwards, apperception takes place. But
still in these processes there is neither restraint nor non-
restraint at the time of subconsciousness, or of any one of the
processes beginning with adverting. But if at the moment
of apperception there arises wickedness, forgetfulness, lack

of knowledge, lack of patience, or laziness, then there is non-restraint. Such non-restraint is called " non-restraint in the faculty of sight." [22] And why ? Because when it arises the door is unguarded, and so also the subconsciousness and the thought-processes beginning with adverting. Like what ? Just as although the interior of houses, door-entrances and chambers, and so forth, may be well closed, yet when the four doors in a town are not closed, all treasure within the town is unguarded, unprotected, so that thieves entering by a door of the town may do what they please, so when wickedness and so forth arise at apperception, when non-restraint is present thereat, the door is unguarded, and so also are the subconsciousness and the thought-processes beginning with adverting. But when virtue and so on arise at apperception, the door is guarded, and so also are the subconsciousness and the thought-processes beginning with adverting. Like what ? Just as, although the interior of houses and so on may not be closed, yet when the doors of the town are well closed, all treasure within the town is well guarded, well protected, and there is no entrance for thieves through the closed doors of the town, so, when virtue and so forth arise at apperception, the door is guarded and so also are the subconsciousness and the thought-processes beginning with adverting. Hence, although it arises at the apperceptional moment, it is said to be restraint in the faculty of sight. And the same with, " when he hears a sound with his ear," and so on. And thus briefly, virtue as restraint of the controlling faculties should be understood as possessing the characteristic of not being entranced by such outward signs and so on in following the corruptions in visible objects, and so forth.

5 (iv, *c*). Virtue as Purity of Livelihood.

Passing now to virtue as Purity of Livelihood (p. 19), spoken of immediately after virtue as restraint of the controlling faculties:—" Of the six precepts enacted for the sake of livelihood " means—for the sake of, on account of livelihood, one with evil desires, oppressed by desire, lays claim untruly, falsely, to possession of a quality pertaining only to the highest kind of men,[1] whereby he commits a Pārājika offence.[2] For the sake of, on account of livelihood, one acts as go-between, and so commits the Sanghādisesa offence. For the sake of, on account of livelihood, one knowingly proclaims (for gain) that a certain brother who lives in one's monastery is a saint, and so commits the Thullaccaya offences. For the sake of, on account of livelihood, a brother, not being ill, demands for his own benefit and eats delicious food, and so commits the Pācittiya offence. For the sake of, on account of livelihood, a sister, not being ill, demands for her own benefit and eats delicious food, and so commits the Pāṭidesaniya offence. For the sake of, on account of livelihood, one not being ill, demands for one's own benefit, soup or rice,[3] [23] and so commits the Dukkaṭa offence,—thus are laid down these six precepts in the words, " Of these six precepts, and so on."

Of ' trickery,' and so on, this is the Pali text:[4] ' *What here is "trickery?" The adjusting, establishing, regulating, of the postures, knitting the brows, the state of knitted brows, trickery, its production and its state on the part of one of evil desires, oppressed by desire, who relies upon gain, honour, and fame, in what is called his acquisition of the requisites and in his round-about talk (with a show of wisdom)—this is called "trickery."*

'*What here is "boastful talk?" Initial talk, boastful talk, repeated talk, flattering talk, very flattering talk, binding speech, encircling speech, praise, full praise, pleasant speech, fawning, bean-curry talk, nurture (of supporters' children) on the part of one of evil desires, oppressed by desire, who relies upon gain, honour, and fame—this is called " boastful talk."*

'*What here is "insinuation?" A sign, making a sign, a hint, giving a hint, roundabout talk, winding speech on the part of one of evil desires, oppressed by desire, who relies upon gain, honour, and fame—this is called " insinuation."*

---

[1] *I.e.* those on the Higher Path to Sanctity.

[2] This and the following five are names of offences against the Vinaya of a descending degree in seriousness, from the first kind which involves immediate and lifelong expulsion from the Order, down to the last which only entails reprimand from a senior brother or sister.

[3] *Vinaya* v, 140.   [4] *Vibhanga* 352 *f.*

'*What here is "crushing slander?"   Abusing, reviling, blaming, sarcastically praising (or casting out), sarcastically praising much (or totally casting out), ridiculing, much ridiculing, accusing, fully accusing, dealing in dispraise, backbiting on the part of one of evil desires, oppressed by desire, who relies upon gain, honour, and fame—this is called " crushing slander."*

'*What here is " hungering to add gain to gain?"   The search, earnest search, full search, the seeking, earnest seeking, full seeking, for one fleshly need by means of another fleshly need, in such wise as taking what has been obtained in this place to that place and bringing what has been obtained in that place to this place, on the part of one of evil desires, oppressed by desire, who relies upon gain, honour, and fame—this is called " hungering to add gain to gain."* '

And the meaning of this Pali text is to be understood thus:—

In the exposition of "trickery," "who relies upon gain, honour, and fame," means, relies upon gain, and honour, and the report of good repute; desiring is the meaning. [24] "Of evil desires" means, desirous of showing off imaginary merits.   "Oppressed by desire" means, set apart by, *i.e.* oppressed by, desire.   After this, because the threefold basis of trickery comes in the Mahāniddesa,[1] as the acquisition of the requisites, roundabout talk, and dependence on the four postures, therefore, in order to set forth this threefold basis, a beginning is made with *in what is called his acquisition of the requisites* and so on, where "basis of trickery that is called his acquisition of the requisites" is to be understood as the admiration of him which causes the presentation to him of requisites in cartloads, since, much as he wants them on account of evil desire, he refuses the robes and so forth offered to him, as knowing also the householders' firm faith in him that he shows favour[2] to those who offer excellent robes in divers ways, exclaiming: " Ah ! what little desire has our master !   He does not want to take anything.   It would indeed be great gain to us were he to accept a little from us !"

---

[1] 224.

[2] Implying that he accepts the gifts offered not because he wants them, but only in order that the donors may obtain merit.

For it has been said in the Mahāniddesa:[1]

" *What is the basis of trickery that is called his acquisition of the requisites?   Householders here below invite a brother to accept the four requisites, namely, a robe, alms, dwelling, and medicine for the sick; and he, of evil desires, oppressed by desire, much as he wants them, refuses the robe owing to his desire for more; refuses the alms, the dwelling, the medicine for the sick.   And he speaks thus: ' What is the use of a costly robe to a monk? It is proper that a monk should pick up rotten rags from a graveyard, refuse-heap, or from shop-refuse, and make and wear his robe.   What is the use of grand alms to a monk?   It is proper that he should maintain life by whatever morsels of food he has received on his begging round.   What is the use of a costly dwelling to a monk?   It is proper that he should live at the foot of a tree or under the open sky.   What is the use of costly medicine for the sick to a monk?   It is proper that he should make medicine out of putrid cow-urine or bits of myrobalan.'   And accordingly he wears a coarse robe, eats coarse food, [25] resorts to a coarse dwelling, resorts to coarse medicine for the sick.   Him the householders know thus: ' This monk is of few wants, contented, secluded, set apart from laymen, strenuously energetic, and ascetic.'   And so all the more they invite him to accept robes, alms, dwelling and medicine for the sick.   And he says: ' Through the presence of three things a faithful son of noble family gets much merit.   From the presence of faith, of the thing offered, and of those worthy of receiving the gift, a faithful son of noble family gets much merit.   You have indeed faith, and there is the gift, and I am worthy to receive it.   Were I not to accept it you would be deprived of the opportunity of earning merit.   I have no need of this gift.   However, I accept it out of compassion for you.'   And accordingly he accepts many robes, much food, many dwellings, much medicine for the sick.   Such knitting of the eyebrows, state of knitted brows, trickery, its production and its state—is known as ' the basis of trickery that is called his acquisition of the requisites.' "*

And the admiration that he excites in various ways by his words, which seem to show his attainment of qualities possessed

---

[1] *Loc. cit.*

by noble men, whereas in truth he is of evil desire, is to be
known as "the basis of trickery that is called roundabout talk."

As has been said:[1]

*" What is the basis of trickery that is called roundabout talk?
A certain member of the Order here below who is of evil desires,
oppressed by desire, and wishful of obtaining praise, speaks
words appertaining to the Ariyan Law, in so doing hoping that
the people may praise him. And he speaks thus: ' That monk
who wears such and such a robe is a powerful monk.' He says:
' That monk who has such a bowl, metal cup, water-filler, water-
strainer, key, belt, pair of sandals, is a powerful monk. That
monk who has such and such a preceptor or teacher, such and
such a friend, acquaintance, companion or intimate friend under
the same preceptor and the same teacher . . . that monk who
lives in such and such a monastery,[2] half-roofed monastery,[3]
graduated turret, flat turret, cave, cavern, hut, gabled house,
tower, square turret, treasury, service-hall, [26] pavilion, at
the foot of such and such a tree, is a powerful monk.' Moreover, being repeatedly blinded by the dust of evil desire, knitting
the eyebrows repeatedly, wonderfully tricksome, excessively
talkative and praised for his words, he utters such speech, pro-
found, hidden, subtle, secret, transcendental, connected with the
Void as, ' This monk has acquired such and such calm attainments of the modes of life.' Such knitting of the eyebrows,
state of knitted brows, trickery, its production and state, is spoken
of as ' the basis of trickery that is called roundabout talk.' "*

The admiration that he excites by regulating his four
postures[4] with a view to getting praise, he being of evil desires
and oppressed by desire, is to be understood as the " basis of
trickery dependent on the postures." As has been said:[5]

*" What is the ' basis of trickery that is called the postures?'
A certain member of the Order here below, being of evil desires,
oppressed by desire, and hoping to get praise from the people*

---

[1] *Ib.* 226.

[2] The roof consisting of two sloping parts which meet at the ridge-
pole.

[3] The roof being one sloping piece.

[4] *Viz.* walking, standing, sitting, and lying down.   [5] *Ib.* 225.

by his actions, adopts an affected style of walking, of lying down, walks, stands, sits, lies down with a resolve to keep up appearances, walks, stands, sits, lies down, as though he possessed concentration, and pretends to be rapt in trance. Such adjusting, establishing, and regulating of the postures, knitting of the brows, state of knitted brows, trickery, its production and state, is known as ' the basis of trickery that is called the postures.' "

In that text (p. 27): " In what is called his acquisition of the requisites " means, in his acquisition of the requisites so-called; or, in that which is said to be his acquisition of the requisites. " In his roundabout talk" means by speech bordering on wisdom. " Of the postures " means of the four postures. "Adjusting" means initial arrangement or reverential arrangement. " Establishing " means the mode of arrangement. " Regulating " means perfect arrangement; it is said to produce faith. ' Knitting of the brows ' is said to mean by way of showing that he is noble and of the first importance,[1] he knits and contracts his brows. His nature is to knit his brows; hence he is known as " knitting his brows." The state of one whose nature is to knit his brows is " state of knitted brows." " Trickery " means wonderfulness. The producing of trickery[2] is " production of trickery." The state of him who works trickery is " state of trickery."

In the exposition of " boastful talk," " initial talk " means that, on seeing men come to the monastery he begins the talk thus: " Sirs, for what purpose have you come ? Is it to invite the brethren ? [27] If so, proceed; I will follow with my bowl." Or it means boastful talk turning upon himself which he makes after presenting himself thus: " I am Tissa. With me the king is pleased. In me such and such a royal high minister is pleased." " Boastful talk " means boasting in the said manner on enquiry being made (as to a good monk). " Repeated talk " is good talk given freely to him from among the householders who is afraid the brother may not be happy in a particular place. " Flattering talk " means talk flattering to such a person as a millionaire, a great

---

[1] *Or,* ' is noble and polished ' *reading* parimaṭṭhita *for* purimaṭṭhita.

[2] *Or,* ' The manner of him who produces trickery.'

boat-owner, a lord of great charities. "Very flattering talk"
means talk flattering a person on all sides. "Binding speech"
means that he talks thus: "Lay-disciples, formerly at such a
time you used to offer the first fruits. Why do you not offer
them now?" And he goes on binding and enveloping them
with his talk until they say, "Sir, we shall offer. We have
not yet had a chance," and so forth. Or, seeing a man holding
a sugar-cane in his hand, he asks: "Lay-disciple, where have
you brought it from?" "From the sugar-cane field, sir."
"Is the sugar-cane there sweet?" "Sir, that may be known
after sucking it." "Lay-disciple, it is not proper to say,
give the sugar-cane to the brother." To him who replies
thus it is enveloping speech, which is "binding speech."
Binding repeatedly on all sides is "encircling speech." The
setting forth with flattery thus: "This family knows me only.
If they have anything to give, they give it to me only," is
"praise," said to be "setting forth." Here the Telakanda-
rika[1] story is to be understood. Praising repeatedly on all
sides is "full praise." Speaking loving words again and
again without regard to anything about the truth or the Law,
is "pleasant speech." "Fawning" is lowliness, speaking
by ever lowering oneself. "Bean-curry talk" bears resem-
blance to a curry of beans. As when beans are cooked some
are not cooked, while the rest are cooked, so when a certain
person speaks, some words are true, while the rest are lies.
Such a person is said to be a "bean-curry-man." His state is
'that of a bean-curry.' "Nurture" [28] is the state of nurturing, the act of him who, like a nurse, nurtures on his hip
or shoulder the children of families—carries them is the
meaning. The state of nurturing is "nurture."
    In the exposition of "insinuation" "sign" is any act of body
and speech producing a sign to others for the giving of the
requisites. "Making a sign" is the making of a sign as much
as to say, "Did you get any food?" on seeing others going
along taking food. "Hint" is speech connected with the
requisites. "Giving a hint" is the production of a hint

---

[1] Telakaṭāhagātha? See *Journal of the Pali Text Society*, 1884, 49 *f.*

thus: On seeing cow-herds tending calves, a member of the Order asks: "Are these calves sucking the mother's milk or drinking diluted buttermilk?" "They are calves sucking the mother's milk, sir," the cowherds reply. Then he says: "They are not milk-sucking calves. If they were milk-sucking calves, the brethren also would receive milk." And in this way he makes the lads inform their parents so that they have to offer milk. "Roundabout talk" is talk bordering on the object wanted. Here the story of the brother, frequenter of a family, should be considered. It is said that a certain brother, a frequenter of a family, enters the house and sits down wishing for food. The lady of the house seeing him, and not wishing to give food, says: "There is no rice," and goes to a neighbour's house as though to bring rice. Then the brother enters the interior of the house, and looking about, sees sugar-cane in a door-corner, molasses in a bowl, flat pieces of salt fish in a basket,[1] rice in a pot, butter in a jar, and comes out and sits down. The lady comes back saying she has not obtained any rice. And the brother says: "Madam, I already saw a sign that to-day my alms-begging would not be successful." "What may it be, sir?" "I saw a snake like the sugar-cane lying there in the door-corner. Looking about with the intention of striking it, I saw a stone like the molasses kept there in the bowl. And the snake, struck by the stone, spread a hood like the flat pieces of salt-fish kept there in the basket. The teeth of the snake wanting to bite the stone were like the rice kept there in the pot. And the saliva mixed with poison issuing from its mouth in its state of anger was like the butter kept there in the jar." Then the housewife, unable to impose upon the bald-pate, presented him with the sugar-cane, [29] cooked the rice, and gave everything, butter, molasses, fish and all. Thus a talk bordering on what one desires is "roundabout talk." "Winding speech" is speaking round and round until one gets what is wanted.

In the exposition of "crushing slander" (p. 28) "abusing"

---

[1] *Read* piṭake *for* paṭike.

is abusing by means of the ten terms[1] of abuse. "Reviling" is humiliating speech. "Blaming" is charging another with fault, such as calling him a person without faith, without belief. "Casting out" (*ukkhepanā*) is casting out a person verbally, saying, "Speak not to him about almsgiving." "Totally casting out" (*samukkhepanā*) is casting out a person by finding a reason, a cause on all sides. Or, *ukkhepanā* means "sarcastically praising," whereby, on seeing a person who has not given alms, a monk calls out sarcastically: "Oho! what a lord of alms!" *Samukkhepanā* is "sarcastically praising much," whereby he calls out: "What a great lord of alms!" "Ridiculing" is making fun thus: "What a life is led by this man who feeds on the seed of kamma!" "Much ridiculing" is making much fun thus: "What! do you call this man a non-giver, who always gives the expression ' nothing ' to everyone?" "Accusing" is charging one with a lack of almsgiving or of praiseworthiness. Making charge thus on all sides is "fully accusing." "Dealing in dispraise" means that he deals out dispraise of a person from house to house, village to village, district to district, thinking that from fear of dispraise that person may give him alms. "Backbiting" means that he speaks honeyed words in one's presence, and speaks in dispraise behind one's back. And because such a speech of one who dares not look another in the face is like gnawing the flesh off another's back, it is called "backbiting." "This is called crushing slander" means, because it crushes, scrapes off another's merits as unguent is scraped off the body with a split bamboo; or because it crushes and grinds to powder another's merits like extracting scent from a fragrant substance by grinding it; and it (this speech) is also a search after gain, therefore it is called "crushing slander."

In the exposition of "hungering to add gain to gain," "hungering" is tracing out. "What has been obtained in this place" means what has been obtained from this house. "To that place" means to that house. "Search" is desiring to

---

[1] *I.e.* calling a person a thief, a simpleton, a fool, a camel, an ox, an ass, a denizen of hell, a brute, and saying to him ' There is no salvation for you,' and ' An evil destiny awaits you.' *Dhammapada Comy.* iv, 1.

get. " Earnest search " means tracing out. " Full search "
means tracing out repeatedly. [30] Here is to be related
the story of the brother who went giving to the boys of
various families whatever had been obtained, beginning from
the first house and getting milk and rice-gruel on the way.
" Seeking " and the others are only synonyms of " search "
and so on. Hence " search " is " seeking," " earnest search "
is " earnest seeking," " full search " is " full seeking"—
thus is the construction here to be understood. Such is the
meaning of " trickery " and so on.

Now in, " Of evil states such as " (p. 19, *c*), by the expression " such as " inclusion should be understood of the
various evil states spoken of in the *Brahmajāla Sutta* in this
way: " *Whereas some monks and Brahmins, while living on food
provided by the faithful, earn their living by wrong means of
livelihood, by low arts, such as these: palmistry, divining by
means of omens and signs, auguries drawn from thunderbolts
and other celestial portents, prognostication by interpreting
dreams, fortune-telling from marks on the body, auguries from
the marks on cloth gnawed by mice, sacrificing to Agni, offering
oblations from a spoon.*"[1] Thus has been indicated this
" wrong livelihood by way of evil states such as the transgression of the six precepts enacted for the sake of livelihood,
and as trickery, boastful talk, insinuation, crushing slander,
hungering to add gain to gain." That abstinence from all
such wrong livelihood is " virtue as purity of livelihood,"
wherein, this is the word-by-word comment: depending on it
people live—" life." What is that? Effort in the search for
the requisites. " Purity " is the state of being pure. " Life-
purity " is the purity of life.

5 (iv, *d*). Virtue connected with the requisites.

And immediately after this there is mentioned " virtue
connected with the requisites," wherein " wisely reflecting "
means knowing on reflection as to expediency and the right
path: considering is the meaning. The consideration mentioned here in such wise as " for the warding off of cold," is

---

[1] *Digha* i, 9.

to be understood as "wisely reflecting." Here "robe" means
any garment such as the waist-cloth. "Accepts" means
enjoys, wears or puts on. "Only for" is [31] an expression
showing the limit of purpose. "For the warding off of cold,"
and so forth—this is the sole object of the religious meditator in accepting the robe; there is no other. "Of cold"
means of the cold arising to any one either internally by the
disturbance of his own elements, or externally by a change
in the weather. "For the warding off" means for the
purpose of warding off; for the purpose of expelling so
that sickness may not be produced in his body. Because
when the body is afflicted with sickness, one becomes
distracted in mind and cannot wisely strive (for culture),
therefore, the Blessed One allowed the use of a robe for the
warding off of cold. And the same with all the other words.[1]
For among them "of heat" means of the heat of fire, *i.e.*,
heat produced in a jungle-fire, and so forth. In "of the touch
of gadflies, mosquitoes, wind, heat, and reptiles," "gadflies" are biting flies, also called blind flies. "Mosquitoes"
are mosquitoes. "Wind" is divided into wind charged with
dust and wind not charged with dust. "Heat" is the sun's
heat. "Reptiles" are those creatures that creep and move
about, such as the long-bodied snakes. Their touch is twofold:
the touch of bite and the touch of contact; and this troubles
not him who is seated covered with a robe. Hence under
these circumstances he accepts a robe for the purpose of the
warding off of such creatures. The repetition of the expression "only for" is to show the limit of a constant purpose.
For "the covering of one's private parts" is a constant
purpose. The others are so only at times. Here "private
parts" means the interstice between the legs. Indeed, when
any of these parts is revealed, the sense of shame is disturbed,
destroyed: and so because they destroy shame they are called
"the private parts." *Hirikopīnapaṭicchādanatthaṃ* means
for the purpose of covering these private parts. The reading
is also *hirikopīnaṃ paṭicchādanatthaṃ*.

---

[1] Occurring in *Majjhima* i, 10, quoted above on p. 20, n. 1.

"Alms" means any food. Any food is called "alms" from its being put into the brother's bowl in his food-gathering. Or "alms" means the collection of morsels of food. It has been said to be the collection, group of morsels of food, obtained from various houses. "Not for sport" means not for purposes of sport like village-boys and so forth; it is said to be "indicative of play." "Nor for intoxication" means not for a display of pride like boxers and wrestlers and so forth; it is said to be "indicative of the pride of strength and the pride of manhood." [32] "Nor for personal charm" means not for the purpose of beautifying oneself like court people and courtesans and so forth; it is said to be "indicative of fulness of limbs, big and small." "Nor for beautification" means not for the purpose of beautifying oneself like actors and dancers and so forth; it is said to be "indicative of clearness of skin and complexion." Of these, "Not for sport" has been said in order to remove the sufficing condition of delusion; "nor for intoxication" has been said in order to remove the sufficing condition of hate; "nor for personal charm, nor for beautification," in order to remove the sufficing condition of lust; "not for sport, nor for intoxication," in order to prevent the growth of one's own fetters; "nor for personal charm, nor for beautification," in order to prevent the growth of another's fetters. And by these four expressions, rejection of unwise attainment and of devotion to a life of pleasure should be understood to have been indicated. The expression "only for" has the meaning already given. "Of this body" means of this material body dependent on the four great primary elements. "For the sustenance" means in order to be stable as a continuous series. "For the preservation" means in order that the procedure (of life-controlling-faculty) may not be cut off; or in order that (the body) may last long. He accepts alms for the sustenance and preservation of the body as the owner of a decayed house props up his house, and a cartman lubricates (lit. feeds) the axle of his cart; he accepts it, not for sport nor for intoxication, nor for personal charm, nor for beautification. Furthermore, "sustenance" is a

synonym for life-controlling faculty. Hence " for the sustenance, preservation of this body " should so far be understood to mean for the procedure of the life-controlling
faculty of this body. " For the allaying of the pangs of
hunger,"—in the sense of inflicting pain, hunger is called
" pangs," for the allaying of which he accepts alms, as one
might accept ointment for a wound, or medicine to counter-
act heat and cold, and so forth. " For aiding the practice
of the noble life " means in order to uphold the noble life
of complete instruction in the Law, and the noble life of the
Path. Indeed, he accepts alms in order to uphold the noble
life, practising, as he does, for release from the desert of existence, by devotion to the three precepts, by means of his
bodily strength on account of his acceptance of alms, as
starving parents might eat their children's flesh in order to
be able to cross a desert,[1] as people who desire to cross a river
rely on a raft, as people who desire to cross the ocean rely on a
ship. " Thus I shall subdue the old feeling and I shall cause
no new feeling to arise " means [33] he accepts alms giving
heed thus: " By this acceptance of alms I shall subdue the old
feeling of hunger and shall produce no feeling due to immoderate eating, like one of those brahmins: one who eats
till he has to be lifted by the hand, or one who eats till his
loin-cloth cannot be retained, or one who has to roll where he
eats, or one who eats till a crow pecks from his mouth, or one
who eats till he vomits." He accepts alms of food as a patient
takes medicine. Or, it is called " old feeling " because it
arises in this life-time owing to unsuitable and unrestricted[2]
food on account of old kamma: " destroying its cause by suitable and restricted food, I shall subdue the old feeling."
And that feeling which will arise in future through the accumu-
lated kamma of inconsiderate eating in this life-time is called
" new feeling." Causing its root not to arise by means of
considerate eating, I shall produce no new feeling,—thus
also is the meaning to be understood. So far should the
compendium on considerate eating, the forsaking of devotion

---

[1] *S.* ii, 98.   [2] *Join* asappāyā *to the following compound in the text.*

to self-torture, and the non-forsaking of righteous bliss be understood to have been shown. "And maintenance shall be mine" means he accepts alms, saying: "By moderate eating I shall have the preservation or equalization called the longevity of this body in harmony with causes owing to the absence of the danger of cutting off the life-controlling faculty or of destroying the four postures." He accepts alms of food as a patient of long suffering accepts healing medicine. "Faultlessness also and comfort"—"faultlessness" is by avoiding inconsiderate search, acceptance, and eating; "comfort" is through moderate eating. Or "faultlessness" is due to the absence of such faults as discontent, drowsiness, sleepy restlessness, and blame by the wise, caused by unsuitable and immoderate eating. "Comfort" is due to the production of bodily strength caused by suitable and moderate eating. Or, "faultlessness" is due to the forsaking of the pleasure of lying down, pleasure of sleeping on the side, or the pleasure of torpor, by not eating food to satiety. By accomplishing the harmonizing of the four postures through eating less than four or five mouthfuls, so that "comfort shall be mine"; thus he accepts alms. Indeed it has been said:

> "*Hath he but eaten mouthfuls four or five,*
> *Let him drink water:—here is sure enough*
> *Refreshment for a brother filled with zeal.*"[1]

[34] And so far the limiting of purpose and the path of the mean should be understood to have been shown.

"Dwelling" means sleeping place and seat. Wherever he sleeps, whether in a monastery or half-roofed monastery, and so on, that is a sleeping place. Wherever he sits, seats himself, that is a seat. The two taken together are called "dwelling." "For the dispelling of the danger of the weather and for the purpose of delighting in solitude"— weather in the sense of causing trouble is "weather-danger." In order that one may dispel the danger of the weather and

---

[1] *Psalms of the Brethren*, 983. See also *Expositor* 511 *f.* for a similar exposition of most of the terms here commented on.

delight in solitude, that unsuitable weather which causes sickness of the body and distraction of mind should be dispelled by acceptance of a dwelling: and it has been said that it is " for the purpose of dispelling that weather and of well-being in living alone." As, although by the warding off of cold and so forth the dispelling of the danger of the weather has been indicated, yet the covering of one's private parts in the acceptance of a robe is a constant purpose, while the others (cold and heat) are so only at times, so here also this has been said concerning the constant dispelling of danger from the weather. Or, this weather as described already is just " the weather." And " danger " is twofold: obvious danger and hidden danger. Of the two, obvious danger is lions and tigers, and so on; hidden danger is lust, hate, and so on. They may cause trouble to one seated in an open yard, at the foot of a tree, and so on, by there being no guarded door and by seeing unsuitable objects, and so on. The brother who accepts a dwelling, knowing and reflecting that there such dangers cannot cause him trouble, is to be understood as accepting it after wise reflection, for the purpose of dispelling danger from the weather.

In " the requisite of medicine for the sick," ' for ' is in the sense of counteracting disease: going against is the meaning. It is a synonym for anything suitable. " Medicine " is the work of a doctor, as being permitted by him. Medicine which is for the sick is " medicine for the sick," said to be anything used by a doctor, such as oil, honey, molasses, and so forth, suitable for the sick. " Requisite " means a protection as in " *surrounded by the seven requisites of a town*,"[1] and so on; an ornament as in " *the (Ariyan) chariot has the ornament of purity, the axle of jhāna, the wheel of energy*," [2] [35] and so on; a constituent as in " *the monk should carry out whatever are the factors of livelihood*,"[3] and so on. Here it is proper to take it as constituent and protection. For that " medicine for the sick " is protection of life, from its guarding it, giving no opportunity for the production of life-destroying disease.

---

[1] *Anguttara* iv, 106.   [2] *Samyutta* v, 6.   [3] *Majjhima* i, 108.

It is also a constituent of life because it is a means of prolonging life. Hence it is called "requisite." And so, being medicine for the sick and a requisite, it is "requisite of medicine for the sick"; and whatever is suitable for the sick and permitted by the doctor such as oil, honey, molasses, and so forth, being requisite of medicine for the sick, is said to be the constituent or protection of life. "Which have arisen" means, which have been produced, have become, have been born. In "connected with diseases," "disease" means a disturbance of the elements, and leprosy, boils, pustules, and so on, sprung therefrom. "Connected with disease" means, because it arises from disease. In "of feelings," painful feelings, the immoral resultant feelings, are intended. "For the freedom from the pain" of those feelings connected with diseases means, in order to be free from the suffering; that is, he accepts medicine until all that pain is removed. Thus in brief this virtue, whose characteristic is judicious use of the requisites, should be understood to be "connected with the requisites." And the word-definition is: Because beings come and go, and live enjoying robes and so forth, relying on these, depending on these, therefore are they called "requisites." "Connected with the requisites" means connected with those requisites. Of this fourfold virtue "the restraint according to the Pātimokkha" is to be attained by faith, for it is accomplished by faith, the enactment of the three precepts being beyond the province of disciples, as is shown by the Buddha's rejection of a request to enact these precepts. Hence observing by faith completely the precepts as enacted, one should be perfect in it (this fourfold restraint), regardless even of life. For thus has it been said:—

[36]   "*Be prudent, reverent ; guard thy virtue well,*
      As pheasant guards her egg or yak his tail,
      Or as a son beloved, or one's sole eye."

And this also has been said, "*So, O king, my disciples do not transgress even for the sake of life the precepts which I have laid down for them.*" And in this sense are to be understood the stories told of Elders bound by thieves in a forest.

It is said that in the Himalayan forest thieves bound an Elder with black creepers, and made him lie down. And the Elder, as he lay, increased his insight for seven days, and attaining the fruition of never-returning, died there and was reborn in the Brahma world.

Again, in Tambapanni Isle thieves bound an Elder with *pūti* creepers and made him lie down. And when a jungle fire came on he established insight before the creepers could be cut, and died in the extinction of his corruptions.[1] Elder Abhaya, a reciter of the Dīgha Nikāya, coming with five hundred brethren saw and cremated the Elder's body and had a shrine built. Hence others of good family also should,—

> Keeping the Pātimokkha pure, let life
> Be yielded up: forsake not virtue's law
> Enacted by the Master of the world.

Even as Pātimokkha-restraint is to be attained by faith, so by mindfulness is restraint of the controlling faculties to be attained; for this is accomplished by mindfulness, because covetousness and so forth do not flow from controlling faculties that are established by mindfulness. Hence, remembering the Fire-sermon[2] preached in this way: " Brethren, better were an iron wire heated, molten, burning, incandescent, aflame, than the faculty of sight grasping details and signs in visible objects," and so on, one should attain it well through checking, by means of unremitting mindfulness, the seizure by the general appearance of visible objects, and so forth, followed by covetousness and other evil states of consciousness which proceed in the eye-door, and so forth. [37] For[3] when it is not attained, virtue as Pātimokkha-restraint

---

[1] Samasīsī—*i.e.* the *head* of his corruptions is severed by the Path of Sanctity when he died. His death being simultaneous with the extinction of his corruptions, he is called jīvitasamasīsī. When one adopts any of the four postures until sanctity is attained and dies in that posture, one is called iriyapathasamasīsī. When one is afflicted with a disease, and attaining sanctity dies of that disease, one is called rogasamasīsī.

[2] *Samyutta* iv, 168.   [3] *Read* asampādite hi.

also does not endure, does not last long, like corn which is not well set round with a thickset hedge. And one is harassed by those thieves, the corruptions, as a village with open gates by robbers; and lust penetrates the mind, as rain penetrates a house badly roofed. And this has been said:—

> " *In sights, sounds, odours, tastes, things tangible,*
> *Guard the controlling faculty : for these,*
> *Finding an open and unguarded door,*
> *Will vex thee as a village vexed by thieves.*
>
> *Even as rain enters an ill-roofed house,*
> *Lust enters the uncultivated mind.*" [1]

But when this restraint of the controlling faculties is attained, virtue as Pātimokkha-restraint also endures, lasts long, like corn well set round with a thickset hedge. And one is not harassed by those thieves, the corruptions, as a village, well closed by gates, is not harassed by robbers. And lust does not penetrate the mind, as rain does not penetrate a house well roofed. And this has been said:—

> " *In sights, sounds, odours, tastes, things tangible,*
> *Guard the controlling faculty : for these,*
> *Finding in thee a closed, well-guarded door,*
> *Will shun thee as a village shunned by thieves.*
>
> *Rain cannot penetrate a well-roofed house,*
> *Lust cannot penetrate a well-taught mind.*" [1]

But this is an extreme admonition. The mind, however, is flighty. Hence restraint of the controlling faculties is to be attained in repelling arisen lust by directing one's attention to the foul, as it was done by the Elder Vangīsa when he was recently ordained. [38] It is said that seeing a woman, lust arose in the Elder but recently ordained, as he was going about for alms. Then he said to Elder Ānanda:

> " With sensual lust I burn, my mind aflame.
> I pray thee, pity have, O Gotama,
> And tell me how I may extinguish it."

---

[1] *Dhammapada* 13, 14.

The Elder replied:—

> " Through wrong perception is thy mind aflame—
> Pleasant appearances avoid, for they
> Are full of lust, but cultivate the mind
> In things unpleasant, that it may attain
> To concentration and a single aim.
> Things-in-the-making shalt thou see and know
> Evil as other than thee, as not the self.
> Slay the great lust. Burn not repeatedly." [1]

And the Elder, repelling his lust, went his way.

Further, a brother who is fulfilling restraint of the controlling faculties, should be like the Elder Cittagutta, who lived in the great Kuraṇḍaka cave, and like the Elder Mahā-mitta, who lived in the great Coraka monastery.

It is said that there was a beautiful painting of the Renunciation of Seven Buddhas in the great Kuraṇḍaka cave. And many of the brethren, wandering round the dwellings, saw the painting, and said: " Sir, beautiful is the painting." The Elder said, " Lads, I have lived in the cave for over sixty years and I did not even know whether the painting existed or not. Now I know to-day through you who possess eyes." Thus it is said that for so long the Elder living there never lifted his eyes and looked up. And at the cave-entrance there was a great ironwood tree. But the Elder had never looked up at it. It is said that he knew that it was in blossom when each spring he saw the filaments that fell to the ground. The king, hearing of the Elder's virtuous attainments, and wishing to pay his respects, sent for him three times. And when the Elder did not come he caused to be shut up the breasts of the women in the village who were suckling infants, and had his seal put to this order: " As long as the Elder does not come, so long these infants must not suck milk."

[39] And the Elder, out of compassion for the infants, went to the village. And the king heard of it, and saying to his ministers, " Go, I say, and introduce the Elder; I will acquire the virtues," had the Elder brought within the palace, paid

---

[1] *S.* i, 188, which gives a different order of the lines; *Th.* i, 1223 *f.*

his respects, gave him his meal of food, and saying to him, " Sir, to-day there is no opportunity. To-morrow I will acquire the virtues," he took the Elder's bowl, accompanied him a little distance, and having, together with the queen, paid his respects, turned back. And the Elder said: "May the king be happy !" whether it was the king that paid respects or the queen. Thus seven days passed. And the brethren said: " Sir, whether it was the king that paid respects or the queen, why did you only say: ' May the king be happy '? " The Elder replied: " Lads, I make no difference as to the king or the queen." After seven days the king, finding that the Elder was not happy there, let him go. The Elder went back to the great Kuraṇḍaka cave, and at night ascended to the promenade. And the deity that lived in the ironwood tree stood holding a torch. Then the Elder's subject of meditation became exceedingly pure and clear. And the Elder was glad, saying to himself, " Why is my subject of meditation so exceedingly clear to-day ?" And causing the whole mountain to resound, he attained Sanctity immediately after the middle watch. And even so should any other son of good family desirous also of his own benefit,—

> Let not the eye wander like forest-ape,
> Or trembling wood-deer, or affrighted child.
> The eyes should be cast downward: they should look
> The distance of a yoke: he shall not serve
> The eye's dominion, like a restless ape."

A poisonous boil once arose on the mother of the Elder Mahāmitta. Her daughter also had been ordained among the sisters. The mother said to her daughter: " Girl, go to thy brother's presence. Tell him I am unwell, and bring medicine." The daughter went and told him. The Elder said: " I do not know how to gather medicinal roots, and so forth, and to prepare medicine. But this medicine will I tell of: since I have become monk I have never broken the controlling faculties with a mind accompanied by greed and looked at a female form. By the virtue of this [40] declaration of truth may my mother be relieved. Go, recite this, and shampoo the lay-sister's body." She went and related the matter, and did as instructed. And in that moment the lay-sister's boil was crushed and disappeared like a mass of foam. And she rose and uttered these words of joy: "If the supreme Buddha were alive, with his hand like a variegated lattice, would he not stroke the head of a brother like my son ?" Hence—

> Another well-born youth having become
> A monk[1] in the religion, he should stand,
> Like Elder Mitta, in the wise restraint
> Of the controlling faculties.

Purity of livelihood should be attained by energy as restraint of the controlling faculties is attained by mindfulness: indeed it is accomplished by energy, because a man of strenuous energy abandons wrong livelihood. Therefore it is to be attained by energetic alms-gathering and so forth, abandoning wrong search and unfitting behaviour, and resorting to those requisites which are clean in their acquirement, and avoiding like poisonous snakes those that are impure in acquirement. Of these, the requisites which a brother, who has not mastered the ascetic practices has obtained from the Order, from a chapter of the brethren, and from laymen who are pleased with him on account of his religious preaching and so forth, are to be known as clean in acquirement. Those obtained by alms-gathering and so forth are exceedingly clean in acquirement. Those which a brother who has mastered his ascetic practices has obtained by alms-gathering, and so forth, and by his regular observance of the ascetic practices, from those laymen who are pleased with him because of his ascetic merits, are to be known as clean in acquirement. The observance of ascetic practice by one who, when putrid sycamore and the four sweet stuffs are sent him for the purpose of allaying a disease, eats only the portion of sycamore, thinking: "My other fellow-monks will eat the four sweet-stuffs," is "fitting behaviour." He, indeed, is called a brother of the highest Ariyan race. Whatever robes and

---

[1] *Read* pabbajitvāna.

other requisites there are, a brother who is purifying his
livelihood should not make a sign, hint, roundabout talk, or
intimation regarding a robe or alms. But a sign, hint, or
roundabout talk regarding a dwelling may be made by one
who has not mastered his ascetic practices. Of these, [41]
when one who is preparing the ground for a dwelling is asked
by laymen: " Reverend Sir, what are you doing ? Who is
enabling you to do it ?" a reply to this effect, "Nobody," or
any similar reply, is making a sign. " Lay-disciples, where
do you dwell ?" " In a graduated turret, sir ?" " Lay-
disciples, a graduated turret is not proper for the brethren."[1]
Such a dialogue, or any other speech to this effect, is giving
a hint. " The dwelling of the Order of brethren is cramped ":
—such talk, or any other to that effect, is roundabout talk.
As regards medicine, all four ways are proper. But is it
proper or not proper to use the medicine obtained in these
four ways when the disease has been allayed ? The Vinaya
scholars say it is proper because the Blessed One has allowed
it. But the Suttanta scholars say that it is not proper because
though there is no offence, yet the life of austerity is spoilt.
Whoso, however, though permitted by the Blessed One, does
not make sign, hint, roundabout talk, intimation, but avoiding
them by virtue of his merits such as contentment, and so forth,
when a mortal disease arises, accepts whatever requisites
are forthcoming, is called, " one who leads an ideally simple
life," like Sāriputta the Elder.

It is told that that senior monk[2] was at one time living
with the Elder Mahāmoggallāna developing the practice of
solitude in a certain forest. To him one day there arose a
wind-disease in the stomach, causing great pain. Late in the
evening the Elder Mahāmoggallāna went to attend on the
senior, and seeing him lying down, enquired concerning the
matter, saying: " Brother, on former occasions how did you get
comfort ?" The Elder replied: " Brother, when I was a
layman my mother mixed together butter, honey, sugar,
and so forth, and gave me undiluted milk-rice; and that gave

---

[1] The punctuation of the Pali Text is incorrect.
[2] *Read* āyasmā *for* yasmā.

me comfort." And the senior said, " Be it so, brother. If
there be merit in me or in you, perhaps we shall get some
to-morrow." And a deva residing in a tree at the end of the
promenade heard this conversation, and thought: " To-morrow
I will produce rice for my lord." And immediately he went
to the family that supported the Elder, [42] entered into the
body of the eldest son, and caused him to suffer pain. And
he showed the means of cure and said to the relatives:[1] " If
you make ready such and such a preparation of rice for the
Elder to-morrow, I will release him." Saying, " You need
not have told us; we always give alms to the Elders," they
prepared the particular kind of rice on the next day. And the
Elder Mahāmoggallāna, coming early, said: " Brother, until
I return from alms-gathering stay here," and entered the
village. The men rose to meet the Elder, took his bowl,
and gave him the particular kind of rice, filling the bowl.
And the Elder showed signs of going. But they made him eat,
saying: " Eat, sir, we give more," and filled the bowl. The
Elder went and offered it, saying: " Now, brother Sāriputta,
eat." The Elder, seeing it, thought: " The rice is very
tempting. How has it been obtained ?" And when he
knew its origin he said: " Brother Moggallāna, the alms
is not fit to eat." And the senior did not entertain such a
thought as: " He does not eat the alms brought by such as I,"
but at the words, took hold of the bowl by the brim, and turned
it upside down, tilting it on one side. And upon the rice
being put on the ground, the Elder's illness disappeared.
Thenceforward it did not arise for forty-five years. And he
said to Mahāmoggallāna: " Brother, even though my entrails
were to come out and move on the ground, it would be improper to eat rice that was obtained on account of vocal
intimation." And he uttered this exalted utterance:—

> Were I to eat the honey-rice obtained
> Through use of revelation made by speech,
> Then would my livelihood be full of blame.

---

[1] *Or,* ' he said to the assembled relatives concerning the means of
cure,' *reading* °nimittaṃ sannipatite ñātake āha.

My bowels may gush out and walk, yet ne'er
For life itself will I break livelihood.
My own mind I control, and the wrong search
Avoid, for I desire not the wrong search
Loathed by the Buddhas.

[43] And here also the story of the Elder Ambakhādaka-mahātissa, who lived at Ciragumba, should be related. So, under all circumstances,

The wise monk, faith-ordained, should purify
His livelihood, nor think of the wrong search.

And virtue connected with the requisites should be attained by wisdom, as purity of livelihood is attained by energy; for it is accomplished by wisdom, the wise man being able to see the evils and the advantages in the requisites. Hence it is to be attained by abandoning greediness for the requisites obtained righteously and justly, and using them only after reflection and with wisdom, according to the rule already laid down.

Here reflection is twofold: as practised at the time of obtaining the requisites, and as practised at the time of using them. Indeed it is using them blamelessly when one uses deposited robes, and so forth, subsequent to reflection upon the elements and upon loathsomeness at the time when they are got, and likewise after reflection at the time when they are used. The latter case furnishes the conclusive decision, for one may use them in four ways: as a theft, as a debt, as an inheritance, and like a master. Of these, a wicked person who uses them sitting in the midst of the Order is using them as a theft. A virtuous person who uses them without reflection uses them as a debt. Hence one should reflect every time the robe is used, and at every morsel of alms received. If one is not able to do this, then one should reflect four times, three times, twice, or once a day, before and after the meal, in the first, middle, and last watches of the night.[1] If dawn

---

[1] *Supply* ekasmiṁ divase catukkhattuṁ tikkhattuṁ dvikkhattuṁ sakiṁ yeva vā paccavekkhitabbaṁ, *after* °yāmesu.

comes before he has reflected he stands in the position of one using them as a debt.

One should also reflect every time one makes use of a dwelling. And in accepting and using medicine also, it is proper to cherish mindfulness. This being so, there is offence if one is mindful in accepting, and is not mindful in using the requisites. But there is no offence if one is mindful in using, after being unmindful in accepting them. For purity is fourfold: admonition-purity, restraint-purity, search-purity, and reflection-purity. Of these, admonition-purity [44] is virtue as restraint according to the Pātimokkha, which virtue is indeed called admonition-purity because one becomes pure through listening to an admonition. Restraint-purity is virtue as restraint of the controlling faculties, which virtue is indeed called restraint-purity because one becomes pure by means of the restraint of mental resolve, saying: " I will not act thus again." Search-purity is virtue as purity of livelihood, which virtue is indeed called search-purity because one is pure of search in obtaining the requisites righteously and justly and abandoning wrong search. Reflection-purity is virtue connected with the using of the requisites, which virtue is indeed called reflection-purity because one becomes pure by reflection as already described. On this account it has been said that there is no offence if one is mindful in using, after being unmindful in accepting them.[1]

The using of the requisites by the seven probationers is known as using them as an inheritance: for these seven are sons of the Blessed One, and so, being heirs to the requisites their father's property, they use them. What! do they use the requisites of the Blessed One, or the requisites of laymen ? Though given by laymen, the requisites are the property of the Blessed One, who has allowed them. Therefore it is to be understood that they use the requisites of the Blessed One. And on this point the Dhammadāyada sutta[2] has been borne out.

---

[1] This sentence is repeated from the previous page, and so should not be marked in the Pali Text as ' *Not traced.*'

[2] *Majjhima* i, 12.

The using of the requisites by saints purged of the intoxicants
is known as using them like a master. For saints, having passed
beyond the slavery of craving, use them like masters. Of
these four ways, the using them like a master, and as an
inheritance, is suitable for all; not so the using them as a debt,
to say nothing of the using them as a theft. And that using
them after reflection by a virtuous person, which is opposed
to the using them as a debt, is also called the using them
like a man freed from debts. This is included in the using
them as an inheritance, because a virtuous man, being endowed
with the training in the higher virtue, is counted as a pro-
bationer. And because among these four ways the using them
like a master is the best, therefore a brother who aspires to
this should use them reflecting in accordance with the various
kinds of reflection already described, and should attain to
the virtue connected with them. So will he be a fulfiller
of duties. And this has been said:—

[45] " *Hearing the Law preached by the Blessed One,*
The follower, who in wisdom doth excel,
Should not without reflection use his alms,
Dwelling, couch, seat, and water to remove
The dust from off his robe. The brother, like
A drop of water on a lotus leaf,
Is not attached to any of these things,
Alms, couch, and seat, and water to remove
The dust from off his robe.[1] *Still mindful, he*
Should of compassion know the mean in food,
Hard, savoury, soft, from donors duly got,
Like growth of flesh in an anointed wound.
Like eating in the desert a son's flesh,
Like lubricating axles, even so,
Should one eat food, never infatuate,
For preservation."[2]

As regards the fulfilling of this virtue connected with
the requisites, the story of nephew Sangharakkhita the novice

---

[1] *Sutta Nipāta* 391, 392.   [2] *Cf. Saṃyutta* ii, 98.

is to be told. For he rightly reflected and ate. As he has said:—

> " As I did eat the boiled and well-cooked rice
> The spiritual adviser spake to me:
> ' Novice, burn not thy tongue through unrestraint !'
> Hearing the spiritual adviser's words,
> I suffered agitation. In that place
> Remaining I attained to sanctity.
> Full of intentions am I like full moon
> Of fifteen days: extinct the intoxicants,
> And re-becoming is not any more.
> [46] Let him then who desireth loss of ill,
> Think wisely and accept the requisites."

So it is fourfold by way of virtue as restraint according to the Pātimokkha, and so forth.

Thus is the particular discourse on the Fourfold Purity Virtue.

(v) In the first pentad of the Fivefold Portion (p. 13) what is to be understood as the meaning is, that these are precepts for the unordained, and so forth. For this has been said in the Paṭisambhidā:[1]

" *What are the limited precepts of purity? They are the limited precepts of the unordained. What are the unlimited precepts of purity? They are the unlimited precepts of the ordained. What are the completed precepts of purity? They are those of good average men, who are applying themselves to the state that is moral, who are fulfilling up to the limit the states for probationers, and who have sacrificed their lives regardless of body and life. What are the precepts of purity not misconstrued? They are those of the seven probationers. What are the tranquillized precepts of purity? They are those of the Tathāgata's disciples who are purged of the intoxicants, silent Buddhas, Tathāgatas, saints, supreme Buddhas.*" Of these, the precepts for the unordained, as being limited in number,

---

[1] i, 42 *f.*

are to be known as "the limited precepts of purity." For the ordained,

> Nine thousand koti's,[1] nine score koti's more,
> And fifty hundred thousand, and again
> Thirty-six (thousand)—are the precepts given
> In the Vinaya Piṭaka by Him,
> The perfect Buddha, and in order shown
> By the brief rule.

Thus, though there is a limit in number, [47] yet these are said to be "unlimited precepts of purity," referring to the fact that one observes them without remainder, and that their limit as measured by the standard of gain, pomp, relatives, limbs, life lies out of sight, like the precepts kept by the Elder Ambakhādakamahātissa, who lived at Ciragumba. Like that senior, so:—

> *Wealth should be given up for a noble limb,*
> *One should give up a limb to save a life.*
> *A man should give up limb, wealth, life, and all*
> *To recollect the Law.*

Not giving up his recollection (of the behaviour) of good men though his life was in doubt, he did not transgress the precepts, and attained Sanctity mounted on the back of a lay disciple through the unlimited precepts of purity. As has been said:—

> " *Not father, mother, kinsman, relative,—*
> *This boon he does thee for thy virtuousness.*
> *Producing agitation, pondering*
> *With wisdom, thou, being mounted on his back,*
> *Hast unto Sanctity attained.*"

The precepts of good average men from ordination are free from the dirt (of corruptions), as soon as consciousness is produced being exceedingly pure like a well-burnished gem and well-wrought gold, and are the proximate cause of Sanctity. Hence the "completed precepts of purity," like those kept by the Elders Saṅgharakkhita, uncle and nephew.

---

[1] koṭi –ten millions.

It is said that the Order of brethren asked Mahāsaṅgharak-khita the Elder, over sixty years old, on his deathbed, about his transcendental attainment. The Elder said: " I have no transcendental state in me." Then a young brother who ministered to him said: " Sir, men have assembled from a circuit of twelve *yojanas* saying that you have entered complete Nibbāna. And the people will feel regretful at your death as an average man." " Lad, I never established insight with a view to seeing the Blessed Metteyya. [48] Therefore raise me and give me opportunity." And the brother raised the Elder and went out. And the Elder, as soon as he went, attained Sanctity, and gave intimation by snapping his fingers. The Order assembled and said: " Sir, dying at such a death-time you have done a difficult thing in attaining the transcendental state." " Friends, this was not difficult to do. But I will tell you what is difficult. Friends, since I became monk, deed of mine done without mindfulness, without understanding, I do not see." His nephew also attained Sanctity after fifty years.

> *If one have little learning, and withal*
> *No concentration in his doing, men*
> *Will blame him both in learning and in deeds.*
> *If one have little learning, and withal*
> *Much concentration in his doing, men*
> *Will praise his deeds, his learning not complete.*
> *And if one have much learning, and withal*
> *No concentration in his doing, men*
> *Will blame his deeds, his learning being complete.*
> *And if one have much learning, and withal*
> *Much concentration in his doing, men*
> *Will praise him both in learning and in deeds.*
> *The Buddha's deeply learned follower*
> *Is bearer of the law. And he is wise*
> *And, as the gold of Jambu, without blame.*
> *Devas praise him, yea, Brahma praiseth him.*[1]

---

[1] *Anguttara* ii, 7.

The precepts of probationers from not being misconstrued by way of views, or those precepts which are not misconstrued by way of the lust of average men, are to be known as "precepts of purity not misconstrued," like those of the Elder Tissa, son of Kuṭumbiya. For that senior, desirous of establishing himself in Sanctity through such precepts, said to his enemies:

> " Breaking both legs I will convince you. Yea,
> I loathe, I am ashamed of death in lust."
> [49] So thought I, wisely pondering, and attained
> To sanctity what time the dawn arose.

Another Elder also, being afflicted with disease, was unable to feed himself with his hands, and was wallowing and rolling about in his own urine and excrement. Seeing him, a certain young man said: " Alas, how painful are your life complexes !" The Elder said to him: " Lad, if I die now I shall get the bliss of heaven. There is no doubt about that. But the bliss obtained by breaking this virtue would be like the state of layman brought about by renouncing the precepts. I shall die even together with my virtue." And contemplating that disease as he lay there, he attained Sanctity and gave explanation to the Order of brethren in these stanzas:—

> " A sickness falls upon me. The disease
> Brings sharp pain and corruption. Very soon
> This body will dry up even as a flower
> Wrapped in hot dust. This ailing, putrid corpse,
> Called loveable, being unloveable,
> Fie on it ! impure thing that men deem pure,
> Full of all loathsomenesses ; loveable
> To the unseeing, this foul-smelling thing,
> Corruptible, void of all purity,
> Whereby intoxicated, dazed, the world
> Destroys the way by which heaven is attained."[1]

The precepts of saints and so on are to be known as " tranquillized precepts of purity " from their tranquillizing of all

---

[1] *Jātaka* ii, 437.

suffering, and from their complete purity. This is purity of precepts fivefold as limited precepts of purity and so forth.

In the second pentad (p. 13) what is to be understood as the meaning is by way of removing life-taking and so on. For it has been said in the Paṭisambhidā:[1] " *There are five kinds of virtue:* (1) *the rejection of life-taking is virtue,* (2) *abstention is virtue,* (3) *volition is virtue,* (4) *restraint is virtue,* (5) *non-transgression is virtue. Virtue is the rejection of theft . . . of wrong conduct in sensual pleasures . . . of false speech, calumnious speech, harsh speech, frivolous talk,* [50] *covetousness, ill-will, wrong views. It is the rejection of sensual desire by renunciation, ill-will by good-will, sloth and torpor by the perception of light, flurry by non-distraction, doubt by determination of states, ignorance by knowledge, discontent by gladness, the hindrances by the first jhāna, initial and sustained applications of mind by the second jhāna, rapture by the third jhāna, ease and ill by the fourth jhāna, the perception of matter by the attainment of the sphere of space, the perception of variety by the perception of aversion, the perception of the sphere of space by the attainment of the sphere of consciousness, the perception of the sphere of consciousness by the attainment of the sphere of nothingness, the perception of the sphere of nothingness by the attainment of the sphere of neither perception nor non-perception, the perception of permanence by retrospection of impermanence, the perception of ease by retrospection of ill, the perception of the soul by retrospection of soullessness, delight by retrospection of disgust, passion by retrospection of dispassion, origination by retrospection of cessation, clinging by retrospection of forsaking, the perception of density by retrospection of loss, reinforcing by retrospection of decay, the perception of constancy by retrospection of change, the sign by retrospection of the signless, hankering by retrospection of the unhankered-after, conviction by retrospection of emptiness, the clinging to and conviction of essence by the higher wisdom of insight into states, the conviction of delusion by the knowledge and discernment of things as they really are, the conviction of attachment by*

---

[1] i, 46.

retrospection of tribulation, non-reflection by retrospection of reflection, the conviction of fetters by retrospection of escape from the round of births, the corruptions occupying the same place with views by the path of Stream-winning, the gross corruptions by the path of Once-returning, the subtle corruptions by the path of Never-returning, all corruptions by the path of Sanctity; virtue is abstention, volition, restraint, non-transgression in regard to all these things. Such kinds of virtue conduce to absence of mental remorse, to gladness, rapture, tranquillity, joy, practice, culture, development, adornment, requisites (of concentration), fulness, fulfilment, certain disgust, dispassion, cessation, quiet, higher knowledge, perfect knowledge, Nibbāna."

And herein, other than the not allowing life-taking, and so forth, described above to arise, there is no state whatever that is called "rejection." And because the different rejections are [51] the support, in the sense of basis, and also owing to their not shaking, the right placing of the different moral states, therefore it has been said previously to be virtue in the sense of being virtuous, already mentioned as supporting and right placing (p. 9). The other four states are mentioned with reference to the procedure and existence of mind as abstaining from this and that, as refraining from this and that, as volition associated with both (abstaining and refraining), and as non-transgression on the part of one who does not transgress this and that. And their being virtue has been mentioned previously. Thus it is fivefold as rejection and so forth.

So far this is the end of the answers to the questions: What is virtue ? In what sense is it virtue ? What are its characteristics, its essence, its manifestation, its proximate cause ? What are its advantages ? How many kinds of it are there ?

6. What is its corruption ? 7. What its purification ?

In what has been said as "What is its corruption ? and what its purification ?" we say that the state of virtue being broken and so forth is its corruption; that its state of being unbroken and so forth is its purification. And that state of being broken and so forth is counted as its breaking conditioned by gain, pomp, and so on, and the sevenfold association with sexual feelings. For a man whose precepts in the group of the seven offences are broken either at the outset or conclusion, is known as having broken virtue, like a garment frayed at the edges. And whoso has them broken in the middle is known as having riddled virtue, like a garment with holes in the middle. And whoso has two or three of them broken in a series is known as having streaked virtue, like a cow the colour of whose body is one or the other among black and red colours and so on mixed with other dissimilar colours, either on the back or on the belly. And whoso has them broken at different stages is known as having spotted virtue, like a cow variegated by dissimilar colours and spots at intervals. And so the state of being broken and so on is due to breaking conditioned by gain and so forth.

And this is by way of the sevenfold association with sexual feelings. For the Blessed One has said:[1]—

" *Brahmin, here a[2] monk or a brahmin is pledged to be chaste and does not actually [52] enjoy a woman, but he likes to have her rub, chafe, bathe, or massage him; he is pleased with it, desires it, takes delight in it. This, O brahmin, is being broken, riddled, streaked, spotted in respect of the holy life. And he, O brahmin, is said to practise impure chastity, and to be associated with the fetter of sexual feelings. And I say that he is not freed from birth, old age, death . . . ill. Again, O brahmin, here a monk or a brahmin is pledged to be chaste and does not actually enjoy a woman, and does not like to have her rub, chafe, bathe or massage him, but he likes to jest, play, and sport with her; he is pleased with it. . . . And I say that he is not freed from birth, old age, death . . . ill. Again, O brahmin, here a monk or a brahmin is pledged to be chaste and does not actually enjoy a woman, and does not like to have her rub . . . to jest, play and sport with her, but he likes to stare and look at her; he is pleased with it. . . . And I say that he is not freed from birth, old age, death . . . ill. Again, O brahmin, here a monk*

---

[1] *Anguttara* iv, 54.   [2] *Read* ekacco.

or a brahmin is pledged to be chaste and does not actually enjoy a woman, and does not like to have her rub . . . to jest . . . to stare and look at her, but he likes to listen to her voice, when she laughs, talks, sings, or cries across a wall or fence ; he is pleased with it. . . . And I say that he is not freed from birth, old age, death . . . ill. Again, O brahmin, here a monk or a brahmin is pledged to be chaste and does not actually enjoy a woman, and does not like to have her rub . . . to jest . . . stare . . . listen to her voice . . . but he likes to think about his former laughs, talks, sportings with her ; he is pleased with it. . . . And I say that he is not freed from birth, old age, death . . . ill. Again, O brahmin, here a monk or a brahmin is pledged to be chaste and does not actually enjoy a woman, and does not like to have her rub, . . . to jest . . . stare . . . listen to her voice . . . think about his former laughs . . . [53] but he likes to see a householder or his son enjoying fully the pleasures of sense ; he is pleased with it. . . . And I say that he is not freed from birth, old age, death . . . ill. Again, O brahmin, here a monk or a brahmin is pledged to be chaste and does not actually enjoy a woman, and does not like to have her rub . . . jest . . . stare . . . listen . . . think . . . see a householder . . . but he likes to practise the holy life in the hope of attaining to a celestial abode, saying, ' By this virtue, vow, austerity, or chastity, I shall become a deva, or one of the devas ; he is pleased with it, desires it, takes delight in it. This, O brahmin, is being broken, riddled, streaked, spotted as regards the holy life.' "

Thus the state of being broken, and so forth, should be understood to be counted as its breaking conditioned by gain and so forth, and the sevenfold association with sexual feelings.

And the state of being unbroken, and so on, is considered as the not breaking of all the precepts, the atoning for those to be atoned, the absence[1] of the fetter of the sevenfold sexual feelings, the not producing of such evil states as anger, hatred, hypocrisy, ridicule, envy, meanness, wile, craft, stiffness,

---

[1] *Read* bhāvena *as part of the preceding compound.*

clamour, conceit, excessive conceit, intoxication, negligence;
and the producing of such qualities as moderation of desires,
contentment, simple life.   Indeed those virtues which have
not been broken for the sake of gain and so forth, or which
have been atoned for even though they may have been broken
through the fault of negligence, and which have not been
oppressed by the fetter of sexual feelings and anger, hatred,
or other evil states, are all said to be unbroken, unriddled,
unstreaked, unspotted.   And they are ' liberating ' through
their bringing about liberation; ' praised by the wise ' through
their being praised by the wise; ' not misconstrued ' through
being not misconstrued by craving and views; and they are
conducive to concentration since they conduce either to
access concentration or ecstatic concentration.   Hence their
state of being unbroken, and so on, is to be known as their
purification.

   And that purification is fulfilled in two ways: by seeing the
evils of the depravity of virtue. and by seeing the advantages
of the fulfilment of virtue.   [54] Of these, the evils of the
depravity of virtue should be understood according to the
Sutta which begins: " *Brethren, five are the evils of depravity
of the virtue of a wicked man.*" [1]

   Moreover, a wicked person, on account of his wickedness,
is not liked by devas and men; is not admonished by his
fellow-monks; is miserable amidst the scoffings at his wickedness; feels remorse amidst the praises of the virtuous; is ill
favoured like a hempen garment on account of his wickedness;
is in touch with pain inasmuch as those who follow his views
bear the pains of the states of woe for a long time; is of little
worth inasmuch as he does not produce much fruit to those
whose gifts he accepts; is difficult of purification like a pit of
excrement that has been collecting many years; is outside
of both (the pleasures of man and of monk) like a vile creeper;
not a monk though pledged to be one, he is as a donkey that
follows a herd of cattle; he is ever alarmed like an enemy
of all men; is not worthy to live with, like some dead body;

---

[1] *Anguttara* iii, 252.

is not worthy to be reverenced by his fellow-monks, even though he may be endowed with such merits as learning, any more than a cremation fire by brahmins; is unable to attain distinction as a blind man is unable to see objects; has no more desire for the Good Law than a grave-digger's boy has for kingship; is in pain though he thinks he is happy, being a partaker of pain as is said in the Fire Discourse.

For in setting forth the visible result of Karma in all its forms, and the exceeding severe pain which arises to evil men with minds giddy with enjoyment of the five sensual pleasures, and the pleasurable taste of the salutation and reverence and so forth which result from these pleasures, the which, merely in recollection, is able to produce heart burning and the spitting of hot blood, the Blessed One has said:—[1]

" *Brethren, do you see this great mass of fire, burning, ablaze, aflame ?*"

" *Yea, Lord.*"

" *What do you think, O brethren ? Which is better: to sit or lie down embracing this great mass of fire, burning, ablaze, aflame ; or to sit or lie down embracing a princely maid, a brahmin maid, or a maid of the householder class, with soft and delicate hands and feet ?*"

" *Lord, it is better to sit or lie down embracing a princely maid and so on. [55] Painful it is, Lord, to sit or lie down embracing a mass of fire.*"

" *I tell you, brethren, I declare unto you, brethren, that it is better for a wicked man of evil nature, of unclean and hesitating conduct, of hidden actions, not a monk but pledged to be one, not a holy man but pledged to be one, putrid within, flowing with lust, offensive as refuse, to sit or lie down embracing a mass of fire. . . . And why ? On this account, brethren, he may die or suffer mortal pain, but on the dissolution of his body after death, it will not make him suffer in states of woe, an evil destiny, in a place of suffering, hell. But, brethren, that a wicked man . . . should sit or lie down embracing a princely maid . . .*"

---

[1] *Ib.* iv, 128 (correct the reference on p. 54, n. 8 of the Pali Text accordingly).

*that indeed is to his disadvantage and pain for a long time;
and on the dissolution of the body after death, he goes to a state
of woe, to an evil destiny, a place of suffering, hell.*"

Having thus by the simile of the mass of fire made known
the pain caused by enjoying the five pleasures connected with
women, the Blessed One in the same way said:—[1]

"*Brethren, which do you think is better: that a strong man
should twist a strong hair-rope round the shins of both legs and
pull it, rubbing them, so that it cuts the skin, and then the thick
inner skin, and then the flesh, and then the nerves, and then the
bones, and having cut the bones, remains chafing the marrow;
or that one (the wicked man) should acquiesce in the salutation
of great princes, great brahmins, or great householders? Brethren,
which do you think is better: that a strong man should pierce
the breast with a sharp spear cleansed in oil; or that one should
acquiesce in the obeisance of great princes, great brahmins,
or great householders? Brethren, which do you think is better:
that a strong man should cover the body with a heated iron-plate,
burning, blazing, flaming; or that one should use a robe, a gift
of faith from great princes, brahmins, or householders? Brethren,
which do you think [56] is better: that a strong man should open
his mouth by means of heated iron tweezers, burning, blazing,
flaming, and throw into it a heated iron ball, burning, blazing,
flaming, so that it burns the lips, and also the mouth, tongue,
throat, stomach, and comes out from below together with the
intestines and the mesentery; or that one should eat food, a gift
of faith from great princes, brahmins, or householders? Brethren,
which do you think is better: that a strong man should seize one
by the head or shoulder and make one sit or lie down on a heated
iron bed or a chair, burning, blazing, flaming; or that one should
use a bed or chair, a gift of faith from great princes, brahmins,
or householders? Brethren, which do you think is better:
that a strong man should seize one, feet upward and head down-
ward, and throw one into a heated iron pot, burning, blazing,
flaming, so that one is cooked giving rise to bubbles, and keeps
on now coming up, now going down, now going sideways; or*

---

[1] *Ib.* 129 f.

*that one should use a dwelling, a gift of faith from great princes,
brahmins, or householders ?"*

Thus under the similitudes of hair-rope, sharp spear,
iron plate, iron ball, iron bed, iron chair, iron pot, did the
Blessed One set forth the pain caused by the enjoyment of
salutation, obeisance, robe, food, bed, chair, dwelling (by the
unworthy).

> Whence can there be true happiness to him
> Of broken virtue, who doth not forsake
> Sensual pleasure, yielding sharper pain
> Than to embrace a mass of living fire ?
> What happiness is there to him whose virtue
> Hath been depraved, accepting salutation,
> Suffering pain more galling than the pain
> Of flesh tormented with strong ropes of hair ?
> [57] What happiness to one who hath no virtue,
> Accepting the obeisance of the faithful,
> The root-condition of a sharper pain
> Than pain of piercing spear ?   Or what to him
> Who knoweth no restraint in use of robes,
> Wherefor he should be punished long in hell,
> Being bound upon a blazing iron plate ?
> Though sweet the food, to one who hath no virtue
> It is as virulent poison: wherefor he
> Shall mouth in hell a red-hot iron ball.
> Though deemed a joy, the use of bed and chair
> By one who hath no virtue is a pain.
> Wherefore let him be racked long time on beds
> And blazing chairs of iron.   And to him
> Whose virtue is perverted, what delight
> To dwell within a house, a gift of faith ?
> 'Mid blazing iron vessels should he dwell.
> Thus the world-Teacher blameth him for one
> Of hesitating conduct, passionate,
> Evil, putrid within, a rubbish heap.
> Fie on the harmful and destructive life
> Of him who knoweth not restraint, no monk,

But wearing a monk's guise and suffering
Austerities !¹   For what to him is life,
Avoided is by the virtuous and good,
As dung by those who would be beautified,
Or corpse.   He is not freed from fears; but freed
From every hope of bliss.   Heaven's door is closed,
The way of hell he hath taken.   Who but he
Is pitiable to the piteous ?
Perverted virtue many faults begets.

Thus by retrospective knowledge are to be understood
the evils of the depravity of virtue.   And the advantages
of the fulfilment of virtue should be taken as the opposite
of the description here given (of the former).

Further:—

[58] His virtue pure, his bearing bowl and robe
Pleasing, his ordination not unblessed.
As darkness enters not the sun, so fear
Of self-blame enters not that brother's heart
Whose virtue is purified.   As in the sky
By the fulfilment of her rays the moon
Shines, in the wood of his austerities
By the fulfilment of his virtue shines
The brother.   A good brother's bodily scent
Brings gladness even to gods: what need to tell
His scent of virtue ?   For it overcomes
The attainment of all other kinds of scent:
Unchecked in all directions it is borne.
Deeds to the virtuous done, though they be few,
Are fruitful.   Thus the virtuous dispense
Honour and reverence.   The intoxicants
Of the conditioning present do not vex
The virtuous.   The virtuous dig up
The root of future ills.
Whatever of attainment among men,
Whatever of prosperity there be

---

¹ *Read* khatam attānaṁ va hantassa *for* chatam°.

Among the gods, it is not hard to gain
By one fulfilled in virtue, if he will.
The attainment of Nibbāna takes away
Burning untold: his mind seeks after it
Whose virtue is fulfilled. Thus should the wise
Show forth the benefits of virtue, root
Of all attainments, various, multiform.

And so the mind of him who shows them forth trembles at the depravity of virtue, and inclines towards its fulfilment. Therefore, seeing the evils of the depravity of virtue and the advantages of the fulfilment of virtue as spoken of above, one should purify virtue with due respect.

So far has virtue been explained in the Path of Purity set forth under the heads of virtue, concentration, and wisdom in the stanza, " *The man discreet, on virtue planted firm.*"

Thus is ended the first chapter called The Exposition of Virtue, in the Path of Purity, composed for the purpose of gladdening good folk.

CHAPTER II

EXPOSITION OF THE ASCETIC PRACTICES

Now virtue, the different kinds of which have been described, is cleansed by means of such qualities as fewness of wishes, contentment, and so on. Because a religious meditator who has kept his virtue should, to be proficient in those qualities, observe the ascetic practices, therefore we will begin the discourse on the ascetic practices, so that he (who observes them) may have his virtue washed and purified by the waters of such qualities, to wit, fewness of wishes, contentment, austerity of life, solitude, loss of sin, strenuous energy, easiness of support by others, and may have his vows fulfilled. And so being absolutely pure in conduct through his qualities of faultless virtue and ritual, he may be worthy of being established in the three ancient orders of Ariyans and, fourthly, of attaining to delight in culture.

Thirteen ascetic practices namely have been permitted by the Blessed One to be kept by those well-born youths who have put away worldly needs of the flesh and who, regardless of body or life, are eager to make fitting progress. They are (1) the refuse-ragman's practice, (2) three-rober's practice, (3) alms-man's practice, (4) house-to-house-goer's practice, (5) one-sessioner's practice, (6) bowl-fooder's practice, (7) afterfood-refuser's practice, (8) forester's practice, (9) tree-rootman's practice, (10) open-spacer's practice, (11) burning-grounder's practice, (12) any-bedder's practice, (13) sitting-man's practice. Therein:—

> As to the meaning, characteristic,
> Observance and directions, grade and breach,
> And eke the benefit of this and that,
> As moral triad, as differentiated,
> In groups and in detail—decision shall
> Be made on these ascetic practices.

[60] Of these, as to the meaning:—

1. A refuse-rag is one which is placed on a refuse-heap in such places as a chariot-road, burning-ground, rubbish-heap, and so on, and which, in the sense of covering-up is like the heap of dust in them. Or, it gets to a loathsome state like the dust—hence refuse-rag; it reaches the loathsome state, as, it has been said, refuse-rag practice means the wearing of a refuse-rag so defined. One who has the habit of wearing it is a refuse-ragman. The practice[1] of a refuse-ragman is refuse-ragman's practice. Practice is said to mean reason. Therefore this practice should be regarded as a synonym for whatever observance by reason of which one becomes a refuse-ragman.

2. In the same way one who has the habit of wearing the threefold robe—namely, the shoulder-cloak, upper garment, and the waist-cloth—is a three-rober. The practice of a three-rober is three-rober's practice.

3. Alms[2] is the falling of morsels as food for the flesh. It is said to be the falling into the bowl of morsels of food given by others. One who gathers alms and seeks it by approaching this and that family is an almsman. Or, one whose duty it is to roam for alms is an alms-roamer, where to roam is to wander. Alms-roamer is the same as almsman. The practice of such an one is almsman's practice.

4. A broken series (*dāna*) is said to be an interruption. An unbroken series (*apadāna*) is without interruption; uninterrupted is the meaning. With unbroken series is *sāpadāna* (*sa-apadāna*), that is, from house to house without interruption. One whose habit it is to go from one house to another in an unbroken series is a house-to-house-goer, *sāpadānacārī*, which is the same as *sāpadānacārika*.[3] The practice of such an one is house-to-house-goer's practice.

5. One-session is food taken at one sitting. One who has the habit of taking such food is a one-sessioner. The practice of him is one-sessioner's practice.

6. Bowl-food is food that falls into a single bowl, a second

---

[1] *Or*, factor (aṅgam).   [2] *Cf.* above, p. 37.
[3] *I.e.* with the addition of the suffix *ka*.

bowl being refused. Now the name bowl-food is given to the acceptance of such food. One who has the habit of accepting such food is a bowl-fooder. The practice of him is bowl-fooder's practice.

7. *Khalu* is a particle with the meaning of denial. [61] Food that is got later by one who refuses further offerings while eating his first meal[1] is called afterfood. The partaking of that afterfood is afterfood-taking. The name, afterfood, is given to the taking of such food. One who has the habit of taking afterfood is an afterfooder. Afterfood-refuser is one who does not take afterfood. It is a name for one who by virtue of his observance refuses additional food. But it is said in the (Great) Commentary: '*Khalu* is a bird which takes a fruit in its beak, but when that falls down does not take another fruit. Such is the man,' namely the afterfood-refuser. The practice of such an one is afterfood-refuser's practice.

8. One who has the habit of dwelling in the forest is a forester. The practice of such an one is forester's practice.

9. Tree-root is a dwelling at the foot of a tree. One who has the habit of dwelling at such a place is a tree-rootman. The practice of a tree-rootman is tree-rootman's practice.

10, 11. And the same with the practices of the open-spacer and the burning-grounder (or charnel-fielder).

12. Any-bed is any lodging that is allotted. It is a synonym for a dwelling first allotted thus: 'This is available for you.' One who has the habit of living in whatever place is allotted is an any-bedder. The practice of such an one is any-bedder's practice.

13. A sitting-man is one whose habit it is to refuse to lie down and to live sitting. The practice of such an one is sitting-man's practice.

All of them are the practices (or factors) of the brother who has shaken off the corruptions through the observance of this and that practice; or, knowledge, which has acquired the common name of shaking-off by reason of its shaking off the corruptions, is the factor for (or reason of) these practices—

---

[1] *The meaning of* pavāritena satā *is brought out in these two clauses.*

hence ascetic practices (or factors). Or, again, they are ascetic because they shake off the hostile corruptions and they are the factors of moral attainment—hence ascetic practices. So far is the decision to be known from the meaning.[1]

And the will to observe is the characteristic of them all. It is also said (in the Commentary): ' It is the person that observes. Mind and mental properties are the states by which he observes. It is the ascetic practice that is the will to observe. It is the physical basis that is rejected.' And all of them have the slaying of worldly lust as function, the freedom from such lust as manifestation, and such Ariyan states as fewness of wishes and so on as proximate cause. [62] Thus is the decision to be known from the characteristic and so on.

As to the five topics: their observance, directions, and others,[2] —in the lifetime of the Blessed One all the ascetic practices had to be observed under him; after his decease, under the Chief Disciple; he being absent, under a saint purged of the intoxicants—and so on, under a never-returner—a once-returner—a stream-winner—a scholar of the three Piṭakas—a scholar of two Piṭakas—a scholar of one Piṭaka—a scholar of one Nikāya —a scholar of one Ágama[3]—a teacher of commentaries—a master of the ascetic practices; and in the absence of this last person one should sweep the shrineyard, sit on the hams, and observe the practices as though uttering them under the tuition of the Supreme Buddha. But it behoves one to observe them also by oneself. And here as regards fewness of wishes by reason of the ascetic practices, the story of the senior of the two brothers, Elders living on Mount Cetiya, should be told.[4]

This so far is the general discourse.

---

[1] Dhutanga: from dhu: to shake off.

[2] See the verse on p. 66.

[3] Ekāgamassa, meaning the same as the preceding, is omitted by the Ṭīkā.

[4] He, it is said, was one who never lay down, but none knew of it. One night as he sat on a bench his brother saw him by lightning-flash and asked if he was practising the habit of the sitting-man. The Elder, through fewness of wishes by reason of his ascetic practice, at once lay down, but afterwards resumed the habit.—*Ṭīkā.*

1. *The Refuse-Ragman's Practice.*

Now we shall set forth the observance, directions, grade, breach, and advantage of each in order.

And first, the refuse-ragman's practice is observed with one or other of the two expressions: I refuse a robe given by a householder; I observe the refuse-ragman's practice. So far this is the (formula of) observance. And he who observes this practice should pick up one or other of these rags, namely, burning-ground-rag, shop-rag, street-rag, rubbish-heap-rag, childbirth-rag, bath-rag, bathing-place-rag, after-return-rag, burnt-rag, cattle-bitten-rag, ant-bitten-rag, mouse-gnawed-rag, side-torn-rag, border-torn-rag, flag-rag, oblation-rag, monk's-rag, consecration-rag, psychic-power-rag, road-rag, wind-blown-rag, spirit-rag, ocean-rag. Tearing the rag he should throw away the rotten parts and wash the good parts and make a robe of them, and wear it after removing his old householder's robe.

As to these, burning-ground-rag is a rag cast away in the burning-ground. Shop-rag is a rag thrown away at a shop-door. Street-rag is a rag thrown into the street from a window by those who desire merit. Rubbish-heap-rag is [63] a rag thrown away at a rubbish-heap. Childbirth-rag is a cloth thrown away after wiping the impurities of the womb at childbirth. It is said that the mother of Tissa the minister had the impurities of her womb wiped with a cloth worth a hundred coins, and had it thrown on the Tālaveli Road[1] in the hope that refuse-ragmen would pick it up; and the brethren took of it just enough for mending purposes.[2] Bath-rag is a rag which sick people[3] throw away as inauspicious when, with the advice of exorcists, they have washed their heads and bathed themselves. Bathing-place-rag is a cloth thrown away at the river bathing-place. After-return-rag is a cloth which men, on their return from the burning-ground, throw away after their bath. Burnt-rag is a cloth partially

---

[1] A road in Mahāgāma and in Anurādhapura.—*Ṭīkā*.

[2] So as to leave some for others.

[3] *Read* nahāpitā, *as in footnote.*

burnt by fire. That also men throw away. Cattle-bitten-rag and the next four are obvious, *i.e.* rags bitten by cattle, by white ants, by mice, torn at the side, and at the border. Those also men throw away. As regards the flag-rag—sailors embark on a boat after planting a banner (at the port); one may take it when they get out of sight. That banner planted on the battlefield by soldiers one may also take, when both armies have marched away. Oblation-rag is a cloth which is wrapped round an anthill and offered to spirits. Monk's-rag is a robe belonging to a brother. Consecration-rag is a robe thrown away at the place where the king was anointed. Psychic-power-rag is a robe made by a newly initiated brother.[1] Road-rag is a cloth thrown away (or fallen) on the road. But one should wait awhile before picking up that cloth, which the owner dropped through inadvertence. Wind-blown-rag is a cloth which, carried by the wind, has fallen afar. That also one may take when the owner is not in sight. Spirit-rag is a cloth given by devas, like the one given to the Elder Anuruddha.[2] Ocean-rag is a cloth thrown up on to the land by the waves of the sea. But that robe which is given with the expression, ' we give it to the Order,' or that which is obtained by monks who go to receive a gift of cloth and alms is not a refuse-rag. As for a robe given by a brother, that which is given out of regard for (the ragman's) seniority, or that which is offered to (the inmates of) a monastery is not a refuse-rag. That which is given out of regard, not for the ragman's seniority (but, for the donor's seniority), is a refuse-rag. And here also that robe which, having been placed at a brother's feet by donors, is offered by him into the ragman's hand, is indeed half pure. That also which, having been given into the brother's hand, is by him placed at (the ragman's) feet is half pure. But that which, having been placed at the brother's feet, is by him given to the ragman in the same way[3] is wholly pure. [64] That which, having been placed in the (brother's) hand, is by him placed

---

[1] Ehibhikkhus, *i.e.* ' Come, brother!' the oldest formula of admission to the Order. *Vinaya* iv, 214.

[2] *Dhammapada Comy.* ii, 173 *f.*   [3] *I.e.* by placing it at his feet.

in the (ragman's) hand is indeed not a robe. Thus knowing the different kinds of refuse-rags the refuse-ragman should wear his robe. These herein are the directions.

Now this is the grade. There are three ragmen: strict, moderate, and soft. Of them he who picks up a rag thrown away in the burning-ground[1] is a strict man. He who picks up a rag[2] which was placed with the verbal expression: ' the monk will pick it up ' is a moderate man.[3] He who accepts a rag placed at his feet (by a monk) is a soft man. And the ascetic practice of any of them is broken the moment he accepts, through his own wish or through submission to a request, a robe given by a householder.[4] This herein is the breach.

Now these are the advantages: The state of his having behaved in accordance with the spiritual guidance (of his superior) as said thus: ' *He is a monk having a refuse-rag as his resource for clothing ;*'[5] his establishment in the first order of Ariyans; the absence of the trouble of looking after his robe; the independence of livelihood; the absence of danger from thieves; the absence of the lust for enjoyment; the fitness of the rag as a monk's robe; the state of its being a requisite praised by the Buddha as ' *cheap, easy to get, and faultless* ';[6] its delightfulness; the yielding of the fruit of fewness of wishes and so forth; the development of right conduct; the institution of a precedent for future generations of monks.

---

[1] The particle *yeva* is used in a collective sense to include the other twenty-two rags.

[2] *I.e.* any of the twenty-three kinds.

[3] But the *Visuddhimaggadīpanī* inclines to the view that he is a strict man because, in the case of the burning-ground, of the loathsomeness of the place and, in the case of rags gnawed by mice and so forth or burnt by fire, of the discarded nature of the rags themselves.

[4] ' But if he accepts it out of regard for the donor's faith and with the intention of presenting it to another, as Ānanda accepted a robe from King Pasenadi for another, there is no breach.'—*Cūḷaṭīkā*. ' It is not proper for a monk to accept a robe which a layman has placed at his feet requesting him to receive it as a special favour. But if the donor goes off dropping it with indifference at the monk's feet saying " He will not take it even when I offer it so," it is proper to pick it up.'—*Gaṇṭhi*.

[5] *Vinaya* i, 58.   [6] *Aṅguttara* ii, 26.

As in the battle shines the mail-clad prince,
So in the routing of the Tempter's ranks
Shines the ascetic in a cast-off clout.
The cast-off clout that the world's Teacher wore,
Rejecting fairest robes of Kāsi silk,
Who will not wear ? Let Brethren take delight
In the old clout befitting hermit ways,
Remembering their vows.

This so far is the setting forth of the observance, directions, grade, breach, and advantage in the refuse-ragman's practice.

2. *The Three-Rober's Practice.*

Next comes the three-rober's practice observed with one or other of the expressions: I refuse a fourth robe;[1] I observe the three-rober's practice. [65] He who observes this practice should, on getting a new piece of cloth, put it by as long as he cannot make it coarse, or cannot find one who knows how to cut it, or lacks any of the articles such as a needle. There is no fault in putting it by. But he should not put it by once it is dyed. He would then become a thief of the ascetic practice. These are the directions.

There are also three grades of men here. When the time for dyeing comes, the strict man, having first dyed either his waist-cloth or upper garment, should wear the one he has dyed and then dye the other. And having put on his upper garment he should dye the shoulder-cloak. But he should not put on the shoulder-cloak. This is his duty in a village-monastery. But in his forest-abode he may wash both the garments together and dye them. In so doing he should sit in a place near enough for him to be able, in case he should see any one, to drag the yellow robe and cover himself with it. For the moderate man there is in the dyeing hall a yellow dyeing robe which he should wear or put on and do the work of dyeing. The soft man may wear or put on the robes which are for the

---

[1] *I.e.* for the purpose of wearing either as an inner or outer garment. It does not refer to a robe thrown over the shoulder, which is permissible. See below, p. 74, n. 2.

common use of the brethren and do the work of dyeing. Even a bed-cover[1] there is proper for him, but he may not take it about with him. Nor may he wear off and on a robe which is for the common use of the brethren. To one who is observing the three-rober's practice a yellow shoulder-cloth as a fourth piece[2] is permitted. It must be one span in breadth and three cubits[3] in length. But the moment a fourth garment is accepted by these three men, the ascetic practice is broken. This herein is the breach.

Now these are the advantages: The brother who is a three-rober is contented with the body-protecting robe, therefore he takes it about with him as a bird carries its wings. And such advantages as these are attained: little need of tendance; the not having to treasure up clothes; lightness in travelling; abandonment of the lust for extra robes; simplicity of life through a limit being set for what is proper; the yielding of fewness of wishes and so forth.

> [66] The wise recluse, who wears the threefold robe,
>   Forsakes a craving for an extra cloak.
> No other clothes he needs to treasure up;
> He knows what taste contented bliss bestows.
> So he, the good recluse, who loves to roam
>   With his three robes, as flies the bird with wings,
> Should note with joy the rule concerning robes.

This is the setting forth of the observance, directions, grade, breach, and advantage in the three-rober's practice.

3. *The Almsman's Practice.*

The almsman's practice also is observed with one or other of the expressions: I refuse an excessive amount of food; I observe the almsman's practice. He who observes this practice should not accept these fourteen kinds of food, namely, food offered to the Order as a whole, to one or more particular monks, food given by invitation, by tickets, food

---

[1] A shoulder-cloth (not usually worn as a garment) for self or another, used as a bed-sheet in the monastery.—*Ṭīkā.*

[2] See note [1] (p. 73).   [3] *Read* ti-hatthaṁ.

given on a day of the waning or waxing of the month, on a
sacred day, on the first day of the moonlit fortnight, food given
to guests, to monks about to travel, to the sick, to those
who minister to the sick, food given in honour of a monastery,
at a principal house, food given by donors in turn. But if
donors do not use the expression ' Partake of food that has
been offered to the Order,' but say, ' The Order partakes of
food in our house; may you also partake of it,' it is proper
to accept such food. Food obtained from the Order and
distributed by tickets for purposes[1] other than the gratification
of fleshly needs, and food cooked in a monastery are also
permissible. These are the directions.

There are also three grades of men here. Of them the
strict man accepts food brought both from in front and from
behind. He gives the bowl to the people who receive it outside their door. He also accepts food given after he has sat
down to eat in the dining-hall[2] after his almsround. But he
does not accept food (that has been promised) by sitting for
it the whole day long. The moderate man accepts food sitting
and waiting for it the whole day; but does not consent to a
meal for the morrow. The soft man consents to a meal for
the morrow and also for the day after. The latter two men
do not get the bliss of independent life; the strict man gets
it. Suppose there is (a sermon on) the lineage of the Ariyans
in a certain village. The strict man says to the other two:
' Friends, let us go to hear the Law.' One of them replies:
' Sir, I have been made to sit for a meal by such and such a
man;' and the other says: ' Sir, I have consented to to-morrow's
meal offered by a certain man.' Thus both of them fail to
hear the Law. But the strict man goes early for alms and
enjoys the taste of the Law. [67] The moment these three
men accept extra food, such as food for the Order and so on,
their ascetic practice is broken. This herein is the breach.

Now these are the advantages: The state of his having
behaved in accordance with the spiritual guidance (of his
superior) as said thus: ' *He is a monk having morsels of alms*

---

[1] Such as medicinal purposes.
[2] Āsanasālāyaṃ bhuñjanatthāya nisinno—adds the *Cūḷaṭīkā.*

as his resource for food ;[1] establishment in the second order of
Ariyans; independence of livelihood; the state of the food
being a requisite praised by the Blessed One as ' *cheap, easy
to get, and faultless ;*'[2] the state of his having overcome idleness;
the purity of livelihood; the fulfilment of his probationary
conduct; the state of not being nourished by others; the doing
favour to the poor (donor);[3] rejection of conceit; checking of
the lust for tasty food; freedom from offence against the
precepts concerning a meal for several monks, a meal subsequent to the acceptance of a previous one, and personal
behaviour; conduct in conformity with few wishes and so
forth; development of right conduct; favour to future generations.[4]

> Contented with his lumps of alms,
> And independent in his life,
> The monk forsakes a lust for food,
> And goes at will to any place.
> His idleness he drives away;
> His livelihood is purified.
> And so the wise should ne'er despise
> The going round to beg for alms.

For such

> A brother going on his begging round,
> Supporting self, not others—him the gods
> Admire; for he is free from gain and fame.

This is the setting forth of the observance, directions,
grade, breach, and advantage in the almsman's practice.

4. *The House-to-House-Goer's Practice.*

The practice of the house-to-house-goer also is observed
with one or other of the expressions: I set aside greedy behaviour in alms-gathering;[5] I observe the house-to-house-
goer's practice. Standing at the village-gate he who observes

---

[1] *Vinaya* i, 58.   [2] *Anguttara* ii, 26.

[3] Who is thus not put to the trouble of having to give much.

[4] In providing them with a precedent.

[5] *I.e.* greediness shown in passing over houses from which one does
not expect to get food, and going to those houses which offer good food.

this practice should see that there is no danger[1] he is likely to meet with. If there be any such danger in the road or village he should leave that place and go elsewhere. Whether it be at the door of a house or on the road or in the village itself, if he gets no alms there he should go away and not count that place as a village. He should not forsake that place in which he has obtained something (alms). The brother should enter the village quite early, so that he may have time to leave any place he finds unpleasant and go elsewhere. [68] If alms be given him in his monastery, or men meeting him on the road take his bowl and give alms, he should accept it. When in his almsround he reaches a village, he should not go past it. Whether he gets nothing or something from that village, he should go from one village to another in order. These are the directions.

There are also three grades of men here. Of them the strict man does not accept food offered before he reaches a house or after he has left a house[2] or food given after he has sat down to eat in the dining-hall on return from his almsround. He gives up his bowl[3] at the donor's door. In this ascetic practice there is indeed none like the Elder Mahākassapa; the occasion on which he gave up his bowl is well known.

The moderate man accepts food offered either before he reaches a house or after he has left a house, as well as food that is brought after he has sat down to eat in the dining-hall on return from his almsround. He also gives up his bowl at the donor's door, but does not sit waiting for food that has been promised. In this respect he is like the strict almsman. The soft man sits waiting the whole day for food that has been promised. The moment greedy behaviour arises in these three men their ascetic practice is broken. This herein is the breach.

Now these are the advantages: The being ever fresh[4] in his relations with the families; the being cool like the moon;

---

[1] Such as an elephant, horse, and other animals.

[2] *Cf.* the almsman's practice.

[3] So that food may be put into it. [4] *I.e.* not familiar.

rejection of meanness for the families; impartial favour;[1] absence of disadvantages that arise to monks who eat together with the families[2]; non-acceptance of invitations; absence of wish for a meal to be brought; conduct in conformity with few wishes, and so on.

> In coolness like the moon, and ever fresh,
> And faultless in regard to families,
> And free from meanness and partiality—
> This brother is a house-to-house-almsman.
> A prudent man, who wishes here on earth
> To lead an independent life, should look
> With downcast eyes the distance of a yoke,
> All greediness of conduct put away,
> And go for alms from house to house.

This is the setting forth of the observance, directions, grade, breach, and advantage in the house-to-house-goer's practice.

[69]   5. *The One-Sessioner's Practice.*

The practice of the one-sessioner also is observed with one or other of the expressions: I refuse to eat food at more than one sitting; I observe the one-sessioner's practice. He who observes this practice should not sit at the place reserved for the Elder in the dining-hall, but find such a suitable seat as will be available for him. If, before he finishes his meal, his teacher or preceptor arrives, he should rise and pay his respects. But Tipiṭaka-Cūlābhaya the Elder said: ' He should keep his seat or his meal.[3] He who has not finished eating may rise and pay his respects, but he may not resume the meal.' These are the directions.

There are also three grades of men here: The strict man will not accept more, once he has laid his hand on the food, be it little or much. If men bring butter and so forth saying,

---

[1] To rich and poor alike.

[2] *Or,* ' the absence of evil or fault such as familiarity with the donors' families.'

[3] *I.e.* keep his seat and finish his meal; *or* rise up if he has not commenced eating.

' The Elder has not eaten anything,' he may accept them as medicine, not as food. The moderate man will accept more, as long as he has not finished the food in the bowl; he is indeed known as ' limited by food.' The soft man will eat as long as he does not rise up. Inasmuch as he may eat until he takes the bowl to wash it, he is limited by the water with which he washes the bowl. And because he may eat until he rises up he is limited by his sitting. But the moment these three men eat food at more than one sitting, the ascetic practice is broken. This herein is the breach.

And these are the advantages: Freedom from sickness, freedom from bodily ailment, lightness in movement, strength, comfort, the not committing of offence through his refusal of excessive food, the repelling of craving for tasty food, conduct in conformity with few wishes, and so on.

> Diseases caused by eating do not harm
> The monk who at one sitting eats his food.
> Not greedy for sweet tastes he does not let
> His work slacken. A monk should gladly take
> Delight in eating so his food, which makes
> For comfortableness and is the source
> Of joy in purity and simple life.

This is the setting forth of the observance, directions, grade, breach, and advantage in the one-sessioner's practice.

[70]   6. *The Bowl-Fooder's Practice.*

The practice of the bowl-fooder also is observed with one or other of the expressions: I refuse a second bowl; I observe the bowl-fooder's practice. When at the time of drinking rice-gruel curry is offered in a vessel, he who observes this practice should first eat the curry or drink the rice-gruel. The rice-gruel would become loathsome, if he were to put into it[1] the curry, in which there might be rotted fish[2] and so on. And he should eat nothing that is loathsome. Therefore concerning such curry the above statement was made. But

---

[1] *Read* yāguyaṃ.   [2] *Read* °maccha°.

any honey, sugar, and so forth, which are not loathsome may be put into the rice-gruel. He should take just enough for his consumption. He should eat green vegetables, holding them in his hand, or else put them into the bowl. Any other tree-leaves are not permitted, since he has refused a second vessel. These are the directions.

There are also three grades of men here. Except in chewing sugar-cane the strict man may not throw away[1] even such things as he cannot eat. He may not eat separating the lumps of rice, fish, meat, and cakes.[2] The moderate man may eat separating them with one hand; he is known as a 'hand-ascetic.' And the soft man is known as a 'bowl-ascetic.' Whatever he can put into the bowl he may separate with his hand or teeth, and eat. The moment these three men accept a second vessel, the ascetic practice is broken. This herein is the breach.

And these are the advantages: The repelling of a craving for taste of various kinds, the repelling of desire for taste in more than one bowl, the seeing of the purpose and measure of food, the absence of the trouble of carrying various dishes and so forth, undistracted eating, conduct in conformity with few wishes, and so forth.

> The bowl-food-eater, disciplined enough
> To delve the roots of taste-desire, with eyes[3]
> Of downward gaze, is not distracted by
> More dishes than his own. With joyful heart
> He bears contentedness as though it were
> A thing that's visible. Who else, forsooth,
> Can eat his food as does the bowl-foodman?

This is the setting forth of the observance, directions, grade, breach, and advantage in the bowl-fooder's practice.

---

[1] Into a second bowl, which, even for the purpose of receiving such things (like fish-bone, grain, and so on), as one does not eat, is not permissible.

[2] Lest he should relish the individual taste of each.

[3] *Read* °locano.

[71]   7. *The Afterfood-Refuser's Practice.*

The practice of the afterfood-refuser also is observed with one or other of the expressions: I refuse extra food; I observe the afterfood-refuser's practice. Once he has made his vow (*pavāraṇā*), he who observes this practice should not eat any more food that may be offered. These are the directions.

There are also three grades of men here. Because his vow applies not to the first almsfood but to the refusal of more food while he is eating it, therefore the strict man who has made his vow does not eat a second almsfood after his first. The moderate man finishes the meal on which he has made his vow. But the soft man eats as long as he does not rise up. The moment these three men accept and eat after their vow any more food that may be offered, the ascetic practice is broken. This herein is the breach.

And these are the advantages: Distance from the offence as to extra food, absence of a full stomach, absence of absorption in the fleshly needs, absence of search for fresh food, conduct in conformity with few wishes, and so on.

> The wise ascetic, who refuses food
> Additional, knows not the pain of search;
> He makes no storage of his fleshly needs;
> He suffers not his stomach to be full.
> To shake off faults ascetics should observe
> This practice, which produces qualities
> Such as increased contentment, and is praised
> By Him the Happy One.

This is the setting forth of the observance, directions, grade, breach, and advantage in the afterfood-refuser's practice.

8. *The Forester's Practice.*

The practice of the forester also is observed with one or other of the expressions: I refuse a village-dwelling; I observe the forester's practice. He who observes this practice should leave a village-dwelling and be in the forest at dawn. Here a village-dwelling is a (dwelling in a) village including its precincts. A village may consist of one or more houses, may or may not have a wall, may be inhabited or uninhabited.[1] Even a caravan that is encamping for more than four months is a village. [72] Supposing a walled village has two gate-pillars like those of Anurādhapura, an outward stonethrow of a strong man of middle height from between the two pillars is village precinct. The Vinaya scholars decide the boundary by taking the characteristic (standard) throw to be the fall of a stone, thrown by young men stretching out their arms in a display of strength. But the Suttanta scholars say that the boundary is the fall of a stone thrown to drive away a crow. In a village which has no wall a woman, standing at the door of the house which is outermost of all, throws water from a jar; the place where the water falls is house-precinct; whence a stonethrow in the way described above is a village. Another stonethrow (from the village) is the village precinct. And in the Vinaya explanation a forest is said to be all that is outside of village and village-precinct. In the Abhidhamma explanation[2] it is forest when one goes out by the gate pillars. But regarding this ascetic practice in the Suttanta explanation this is the characteristic measure: a forest-dwelling is at least 500 bow-lengths (or fathoms) distant. That distance is to be measured and fixed by means of a drawn standard bow[3] from the gate pillars, if the village has a wall, or from the first stone-throw if the village has no wall, as far as the monastery-wall.

The Vinaya Commentaries say that if the monastery has no wall, the limit of the measure is the first dwelling, dining hall, permanent assembly hall, Tree of Wisdom or shrine, provided these are far from the monastery, But the Majjhima Commentary says that after fixing the precinct of the monastery as in the case of the village[4] the measure is to be made between the two stonethrows.[5] This is the measure to be taken here.

---

[1] *Or*, inhabited by unhuman beings. On the definitions here see *Vinaya* iii, 46.

[2] *Vibhanga* 251.   [3] *Lit.* ' master-bow.'

[4] *I.e.* a strone-throw to drive away a crow.

[5] One to fix the monastery-precinct and the other the village-precinct.

If the village be so near that those in the monastery could hear the voices of the villagers, and yet it could not be reached by a straight path on account of such obstacles as hills, rivers, and so on, and if the natural means of approach be to cross by a boat, then the measure of 500 bow-lengths is to be taken by that (watery) path. Whosoever blocks the way here and there, so that the requisite measure may be fulfilled, is a thief of the ascetic practice.

And if the forester's preceptor or teacher be ill and the necessary medicine cannot be obtained in the forest, [73] he may then take the sick man to a village-dwelling and look after him. But he should depart in good time, so that at dawn he may be in a place which fulfils the requirements of his practice.

If at dawn their illness increases, he should do his duty by them and pay no heed to the purity of his ascetic practice. These are the directions.

There are also three grades of men here: The strict man should find the dawn break in the forest at all times. The moderate man is allowed to live in the village for the four months of rain; the soft man for the four months of winter as well. The ascetic practice is not broken, if the dawn breaks while these three men, having come from the forest during their terms of forest-life, listen to the Law in a village-dwelling. It is not broken though the dawn may break, while they are still on their way back from the sermon. But if after the preacher has risen up they go to sleep saying ' We will lie down awhile and then depart,' and the dawn breaks, or if out of enjoyment they let the day dawn upon them in the village-dwelling, then the ascetic practice is broken. This herein is the breach.

And these are the advantages: The forester-brother who attends to the perception of the forest can acquire concentration not yet acquired or keep that which has been acquired. The teacher also is pleased with him, as He has said: ' *Nāgita, I am pleased with the forest-life of that brother.*'[1] Improper

---

[1] *Anguttara* iii, 343.

objects and so forth do not distract the mind of him who lives
in a border-dwelling; he is free from fear; he puts away a
craving for life, enjoys the taste of the bliss of solitude; the
practices of the refuse-ragman and others are also agreeable
to him.

> Secluded, solitary, delighting in
> A border-dwelling, by his forest-life
> The monk endears himself unto the Lord.
> Alone in forest-life, he gets that bliss,
> Whose taste even gods with Inda do not get.
> The refuse-rag he wears as coat of mail;
> The signs of other practices he wears
> As weapons.[1]   At the forest battle-ground
> He conquers ere long Māra and his hosts.
> So should the wise delight in forest-life.

This is the setting forth of the observance, directions,
grade, breach, and advantage in the forester's practice.

[74]   9. *The Tree-Rootman's Practice.*

The practice of the tree-rootman also is observed with one or
other of the expressions: I refuse a covered dwelling; I observe
the tree-rootman's practice. He who observes this practice
should avoid these trees: a tree which grows on the border
between two countries, a sacred tree, a resinous tree, a fruit
tree, a tree on which bats live, a hollow tree, a tree growing
in the middle of a monastery. He should resort to a tree on
the oustkirt of a monastery. These are the directions.

There are also three grades of men here: The strict man is
not allowed to resort to any tree he pleases and make a clearing
underneath it. He may dwell under a tree after removing
with his foot the fallen leaves. The moderate man is allowed
to cause those who arrive at the tree to make a clearing. The
soft man may summon the monastery-lads and ask them to
make a clearing, to level it, to scatter sand on it, to make an
enclosure and to fix a door, and may dwell there. On a feast

---

[1] *Read* yudho *as part of the preceding compound.*

day the ascetic should not remain at the foot of the tree but go to some other hidden place and sit down. The moment these three men make a dwelling in a covered place, their ascetic practice is broken. Reciters of the Anguttara Nikāya say that it is broken the moment they consciously let the day dawn upon them in a covered dwelling. This herein is the breach.

Now these are the advantages: Attainment in accordance with the third requisite as expressed in, '*A monk depending on a dwelling at the foot of a tree;*'[1] the possession of requisites praised by the Blessed One thus, '*They are trifling,*[2] *easily got, and faultless;*'[3] the production of the perception of impermanence by seeing the constant change in tender leaves, the absence of meanness for a dwelling[4] and of delight in new work, intercourse with tree-deities, conduct in conformity with few wishes, and so forth.

> Where is the lonely man's abode, extolled
> By Buddha best of men as requisite,
> And which is equal to the root of tree ?
> The well-controllèd man, who lives at such
> A lonely place, protected by the gods,
> Subdues all meanness for a dwelling-place.
> [75] He sees the change that comes o'er tender leaves,
> Which turn from deep red into indigo,
> And fall as sere leaves to the ground. From this
> He learns the lesson of impermanence.
> Therefore the wise should not despise to dwell
> In isolation at the foot of tree,
> The Buddha's heritage and home of those,
> Who take delight in culture of the mind.

This is the setting forth of the observance, directions, grade, breach, and advantage in the tree-rootman's practice.

---

[1] *Vinaya* i, 58.   [2] As regards care, duty, or tendance.
[3] *Anguttara* ii, 26.
[4] On the five kinds of meanness see *Expositor* 480.

10. *The Open-Spacer's Practice.*

The practice of the open-spacer also is observed with one or other of the expressions: I refuse a roof as well as the root of a tree; I observe the open-spacer's practice. He who observes this practice may enter the sacred house either to listen to the Law or to do the sacred duties. If the rain falls while he is inside he should not go out in the rain but wait till it ceases. He may enter the dining-hall or the fire-hall to do his duties. He may invite the Elders and brethren in the dining-hall to a meal. As an instructor (of the Pāli) or as a pupil he may enter a covered dwelling. He may cause to be brought inside bedsteads and stools which are badly kept outside. If the rain falls while he is going along carrying a requisite that belongs to his seniors, he may enter a hall on the way. If he is not carrying any such thing, he may not hasten with the intention of entering the hall, but going with his ordinary steps he may enter and remain till the rain ceases and then depart. These are the directions which also apply to the tree-rootman.

There are also three grades of men here: The strict man may not dwell depending on a tree, mountain, or house. He should dwell beneath the open sky in a hut made of leaves. The moderate man may dwell depending on trees, mountains, or houses without entering them. For the soft man a cave not covered with a roof, a pavilion of branches, a cloth-cover for a chair, a hut in the field deserted by field-watchers and so forth, are permissible. The moment these three men enter a roof or beneath a tree to dwell there, [76] the ascetic practice is broken. Reciters of the Anguttara Nikāya say that it is broken the moment they consciously let the dawn break upon them in such places. This herein is the breach.

Now these are the advantages: The cutting off of the nuisance of an abode, the dispelling of sloth and torpor, worthiness of the praise bestowed as, ' *Like the deer the brethren live untrammelled in their walks, homeless,*'[1] freedom from attach-

---

[1] *Saṃyutta* i, 199. *Cf. Kindred Sayings* I, 253, n. 3.

ment,[1] the going (at will) in the four directions, conduct in conformity with few wishes, and so forth.

> As free in mind as is the antelope,
> The brother lives an easy homeless life
> Beneath the open sky lit by the moon,
> A lamp that lights the vault of starry gems.
> His torpid sloth he drives away and takes
> Delight in culture; presently he finds
> The tasteful essence of his solitude.
> Therefore the wise should take delight in life
> Beneath the open sky.

This is the setting forth of the observance, directions, grade, breach, and advantage in the open-spacer's practice.

11. *The Burning-Grounder's Practice.*

The practice of the burning-grounder also is observed with one or other of the expressions: I refuse (to dwell in) a place that is not a burning-ground; I observe the burning-grounder's practice. He who observes this practice should not dwell in a place which village-builders fix as burning-ground. For when a dead body has not been burnt on it, the place is not known as burning-ground. It is a burning-ground, though it has been deserted for twelve years since a dead body was burnt there. But he may not have there promenades and pavilions and so forth built, bedsteads and stools arranged, water and food brought, and live there teaching the Law. This ascetic practice is indeed heavy. Therefore in order to quell any danger that might arise he should tell the Elder of the Order or one connected with the king, and live free from negligence. In walking to and fro he should do so looking with half-closed eyes at the burning of dead bodies. [77] In going to the burning-ground also he should leave the main road and go by a side path. He should note any object there by daylight, so that it may not appear to him fearful at night. Though unhuman beings may roam about uttering loud cries, he should not throw anything to hit them. He

---

[1] To houses and so forth.

should not pass a single day without going to the burning-ground. Reciters of the Anguttara Nikāya say that after spending the middle watch of the night at the burning-ground he may depart in the last watch. He should not partake of such foodstuffs as sesamum, flour, peas, rice, fish, meat, milk, oil, molasses, that are dear to unhuman beings, nor take them to the houses of donors. These are the directions.

There are also three grades of men here: The strict man should dwell where there are continual burning, continual smell of dead bodies, and continual weeping. The moderate man may dwell where there is one of these present. The soft man may dwell in a place which just fulfils the requirements of a burning-ground as given above. When these three men make their abode in a place which is not burning-ground, their ascetic practice is broken. This herein is the breach.

Now these are the advantages: Attainment of mindfulness regarding death, a life free from negligence, acquirement of the outward sign of the foul, dispelling of sensual lust, the perpetual seeing of the intrinsic nature of the body, growth of agitation, rejection of the pride of health, overcoming of fear and fright, respect paid by unhuman beings, conduct in conformity with few wishes, and so forth.

> The faults of negligence, even while he sleeps,
> Touch not the burning-ground-recluse, such is
> The power of his mindfulness of death.
> Because so many corpses he beholds,
> His mind is freed from lust's dominion.
> Great agitation seizes him and leaves
> Him without pride. He makes a right effort
> To win tranquillity. Therefore with heart
> Inclined unto Nibbāna follow hard
> The burning-grounder's practice, which bestows
> Such manifold merits and qualities.

This is the setting forth of the observance, directions, grade, breach, and advantage in the burning-grounder's practice.

[78]   12. *The Any-Bedder's Practice.*

The practice of the any-bedder also is observed with one or other of the expressions: I set aside greedy behaviour regarding dwellings; I observe the any-bedder's practice. He who observes this practice should be content with whatever dwelling is allotted to him by the distributor who says, ' This is for you.'   He should not oust any man from his place.[1] These are the directions.

There are also three grades of men here: The strict man must not ask concerning a dwelling he has come to,[2] whether it is far or quite near, troubled by unhuman beings, snakes, and so on, or whether it is hot or cold.   The moderate man may ask such questions, but may not go and examine it.   The soft man may go and examine it, and if it does not please him he may take another.   The moment greedy behaviour in regard to dwellings arises in these three men, their ascetic practice is broken.   This herein is the breach.

Now these are the advantages: Obeying the advice given, as: ' *One should be content with what one gets,*' seeking the good of one's fellow-monks, abandonment of thought of what is inferior and superior, rejection of approval and disapproval, closing the door of covetousness, conduct in conformity with few wishes, and so forth.

> Content with what he gets, the any-bed-
> Recluse lies down in careless ease on beds,
> Even though they be of grass.   He does not long
> For what is best, is not perturbed because
> Of an inferior bed.   To younger monks
> He shows compassion.   So a wise man ought
> To be content with any bed, a rule
> Of constant practice with the Ariyas,
> And by the Bull-sage fittingly extolled.

This is the setting forth of the observance, directions, grade, breach, and advantage in the any-bedder's practice.

---

[1] *Or*, he should not make another place for himself.

[2] *Or*, allotted to him.

13. *The Sitting-Man's Practice.*

The practice of the sitting-man also is observed with one or
other of the expressions: I refuse to lie down; I observe the
sitting-man's practice. He who observes this practice should
rise up and walk to and fro for one watch out of the three
watches of the night, for lying down is the only posture that
is not permitted to him. These are the directions.

[79] There are also three grades of men here: The strict
man is not allowed a plank with a back support, or a cushion
of cloth for squatting on, or a bandage-cloth. The moderate
man may use any one of these three. The soft man is allowed
a plank with a back support, a cushion of cloth for squatting
on, a bandage-cloth, a pillow, a five-limbed seat, a seven-
limbed seat. A seat with a back support to lean against is a
five-limbed seat. A seat with a back support and a hand
support on either side is a seven-limbed seat. It is said
that people made such a seat for Mīlhābhaya the Elder, who,
becoming a never-returner, entered parinibbāna. The moment
these three men accept a bed to lie on, their ascetic practice
is broken. This herein is the breach.

Now these are the advantages: The cutting off of mental
bondage described as: '*He lives devoted to the pleasure of
lying down, the pleasure of lying on one's side,*[1] *the pleasure
of torpor,*'[2] fitness for application to all subjects of meditation, satisfied state of the postures, agreeableness for strenuous
effort, development of right attainment.

> The monk who sits cross-legged, keeping straight
> The body, doth disturb the Tempter's heart.
> He takes no pleasure in the torpid state,
> In lying down, but wakes his energies
> And joyfully sits up, illumining
> The grove of his ascetic practices.
> As bliss and rapture, cleansed of earthly things,
> Reward the monk, so one should steadfastly
> Perform the duty of the sitting man.

This is the setting forth of the observance, directions,
grade, breach, and advantage in the sitting-man's practice.

---

[1] *Or*, of turning from side to side. [2] *Majjhima* i, 103.

Of Ascetic and Other Terms as Moral Triad.

Now this is the elucidation of the verse (p. 66):

> As moral triad, as differentiated,
> In groups and in detail—decision shall
> Be made regarding these ascetic practices.

Therein, 'as moral triad' means that all the ascetic practices may be moral or unmoral as those of probationers, average persons and of saints purged of the intoxicants. [80] There is no ascetic practice that is immoral. But the sectary says, an ascetic practice may also be immoral because of the saying: ' *There is a forester of evil desires, not free from desire.*'[1] We reply that we do not say that one may not dwell with an immoral thought in the forest. For whosoever makes his abode in the forest is a forester, who may have evil desires, or little, or no desire. Because the corruptions are shaken off through this and that observance, the practices (or factors) of the brother who has shaken them off are called 'ascetic practices.' Or, knowledge which has obtained the common name of asceticism, because it shakes off the corruptions, is the factor of these observances—thus 'ascetic practice' (or factor). Or again, it has been said that because these observances shake off the hostile corruptions they are ascetic, and they are factors of (moral) attainment—thus 'ascetic practice.' No one whose observances are[2] such factors is known as ascetic on account of his immorality. Else we should speak of ascetic practices of which the factor is immorality which shakes off nothing; and immorality does not shake off greediness for robes and other evil states, nor is it a factor of moral attainment. Therefore what has been said as, ' There is no ascetic practice that is immoral,' is well said. There is no ascetic practice in the ultimate sense to those whose ascetic practice is freed from the moral triad.[3] From the shaking off of what does this imaginary thing become ascetic practice ? They would also fall into opposition with the saying: ' He goes

---

[1] *Anguttara* iii, 219.   [2] *Read* bhaveyyuṁ *for* bhaveyyaṁ.
[3] Because they consider it as a concept.

on keeping the ascetic duties.' Therefore their saying should not be accepted.

This so far is the elucidation by way of the moral triad.

Of Ascetic and Other Terms as Differentiated.

(1) Ascetic should be understood, (2) ascetic doctrine should be understood, (3) ascetic states should be understood, (4) ascetic practices should be understood, (5) for whom is the practising of the ascetic practices suitable ?—this should be understood. Of these points (1) ' ascetic ' is a person who has shaken off the corruptions, or a state for the shaking off of the corruptions. (2) In ' ascetic doctrine ' there is one who is ascetic and not ascetic preacher, there is one who is not ascetic but ascetic preacher, there is one who is neither ascetic nor ascetic preacher, there is one who is both ascetic and ascetic preacher. Of these he who has shaken off his corruptions by means of his ascetic practice, but does not admonish nor instruct others regarding ascetic practice, is an ascetic but not ascetic preacher, like Bakkula the Elder;[1] as has been said: ' *This venerable Bakkula is ascetic not ascetic preacher.*' And whoso [81] has not shaken off his corruptions by means of ascetic practice, but just admonishes, instructs others regarding it, is not ascetic but ascetic preacher, like Upananda the Elder;[2] as has been said: ' *This venerable Upananda Sakyaputta is not an ascetic but ascetic preacher.*' Whoso is deficient in both respects like Lāludāyī[3] is neither ascetic nor ascetic preacher; as has been said: ' *This venerable Lāludāyī is neither ascetic nor ascetic preacher.*' Whoso like the captain of the Law[4] is fulfilled in both respects is ascetic and ascetic preacher; as has been said: ' *This venerable Sāriputta is both ascetic and ascetic preacher.*' (3) ' Ascetic states should be understood '—these five attendant states of the volition of ascetic practice: fewness of wishes, contentment, austerity, solitude, desire-for-these-states are known as ascetic states from the expression, ' depending on fewness of wishes, and so on.' Of them fewness of wishes and content-

---

[1] *Cf. Majjhima* iii, 124 *f.*   [2] *Cf. Jātaka* ii, 441.
[3] *Cf. Ib.* i, 123, 446 *f.*   [4] *Cf. Theragāthā* 982 *f.*

ment fall under non-greed; austerity and solitude under the two states: non-greed and non-delusion. Desire-for-these-states is knowledge. By means of non-greed one shakes off greed for forbidden things, by non-delusion one shakes off delusion which covers faults in them, and by non-greed one shakes off devotion to the pleasure of sense which arises from resorting to things allowed. By non-delusion one shakes off devotion to self-torture, which arises on account of excessive austerity in ascetic practice. Therefore should these states be understood as ascetic states. (4) By ascetic practices should be understood the thirteen, namely, the refuse-rag-man's practice . . . sitting-man's practice. They have been stated as regards their meaning, characteristic and so forth. (5) For whom is the practising of ascetic practice suitable ?— for one walking in lust and one walking in delusion. Why so ? Because the practising of ascetic practice is of painful progress and means a life of austerity; and through painful progress lust is calmed, through austerity the delusion of a non-negli-gent man is put away. Or, herein the practising of the practices of the forester and of the tree-rootman is suitable for one walking in hate, for hate ceases in one dwelling without society in the forest or at the foot of a tree.

This is the elucidation of ascetic and other terms as differ-entiated.

[82]   *In Groups and in Detail.*

' In groups ' these ascetic practices are eight—three chief practices and five unmixed (separate) practices. Of them the practices of the house-to-house-goer, one-sessioner, and open-spacer are the three chief practices. For whoso keeps the house-to-house-goer's practice will also keep the almsman's practice. And whoso keeps the one-sessioner's practice, for him the practices of the bowl-fooder and afterfood-refuser will be easy to keep. Whoso keeps the open-spacer's practice, what need is there for him to keep the practices of the tree-rootman and the any-bedder ? Thus these three are the chief practices. They make eight with these five: practices of the forester, refuse-ragman, three-rober, sitting-man, burning-

grounder. Again, they form four classes: two concerning
the robe, five concerning the alms, five concerning the dwelling, one concerning energy. Of these the sitting-man's practice
is one that concerns energy; the others are obvious. Again,
all are of two kinds by way of dependence: twelve depending
on the requisites, one depending on energy. They are also
of two kinds as to be resorted to and as not to be resorted to.
For they should be resorted to by him whose subject of meditation increases with such resort, but not by him whose subject
of meditation decreases with it. He whose subject of meditation increases and does not decrease, whether he resorts to
them or not, should also resort to them out of compassion for
posterity. For the sake of habit in future they should be resorted to by him also whose subject of meditation, whether he
resorts to them or not, does not increase. Though twofold, as
to be resorted to and as not to be resorted to, all of them are
one by way of volition; for ascetic practice as the volition to
observe is just one. It is also said in the commentaries:
' They say that which is volition is ascetic practice.'

' In detail' they are forty-two:—thirteen for brethren,
eight for sisters, twelve for novices, seven for female student
novices, two for lay-disciples male and female. If there were
a burning-ground fulfilled with the forester's practice in open
space, a single brother would be able to enjoy all the ascetic
practices at once. But the two practices of the forester and
the afterfood-refuser are prohibited for sisters by precept;
[83] and the three practices of the open-spacer, tree-rootman,
burning-grounder are difficult to carry out, for it is not proper
for a sister to live without a second person; and in such places[1]
it is hard to get a second with similar wishes. Even if one
was obtained, the sister would not be free from a life shared
with others. This being so, the purpose for which she resorted
to the ascetic practice would not be fulfilled. So, owing
to impracticability, five of the practices are left out for the
sisters, and only eight are to be taken.

Excepting the three-rober's practice from those mentioned

---

[1] *Or*, on such occasions, under such circumstances.

for the brethren and sisters, the remaining twelve are to be known as for male novices, and seven for female novices. For lay-disciples male and female the two practices of the one-sessioner and the bowl-fooder are suitable and practicable. Thus in detail they are forty-two.

This is the elucidation in groups and in detail.

Thus far is told the discourse on the ascetic practices to be observed for the fulfilment of those qualities, such as fewness of wishes, contentment, by means of which there is cleansing of virtue, the different kinds of which have been shown in the Path of Purity under the heads of virtue, concentration, and understanding in the stanza:

The man discreet on virtue planted firm.

Thus is ended the second chapter called The Exposition of Ascetic Practices, in the Path of Purity, composed for the purpose of gladdening good folk.

PRINTED IN GREAT BRITAIN BY
BILLING AND SONS, LTD., GUILDFORD AND ESHER

CPSIA information can be obtained
at www.ICGtesting.com
Printed in the USA
LVHW081145210223
739960LV00013B/1065